ANXIOUS IN LOVE

How Stopping the Spiral of Toxic Thoughts and
Anxiety in Relationship Overcoming Conflicts and
Insecure of Couple. Abandonment and Separation,
Insecure in Love, Developing Self-Awareness

Teresa Williams Dr Miller Scarlett

© Copyright 2020 by Teresa Williams Dr Miller Scarlett

All rights reserved.

The material contained herein is presented with the intent of furnishing pertinent and relevant information and knowledge on the topic with the sole purpose of providing entertainment. The author should thus not be considered an expert on the topic in this material despite any claims to such expertise, first-hand knowledge and any other reasonable claim to specific knowledge on the material contained herein. The information presented in this work has been researched to ensure its reasonable accuracy and validity. Nevertheless, it is advisable to consult with a duly licensed professional in the area pertaining to this topic, or any other covered in this book, in order to ensure the quality and validity of the advice and/or techniques contained in this material.

This is a legally binding statement as deemed so by the Committee of Publishers Association and the American Bar Association in the United States. Any reproduction, transmission, copying or otherwise duplication of the material contained in this work are in violation of current copyright legislation. No physical or digital copies of this work, both total and partial, may not be done without the Publisher's express written consent. All additional rights are reserved by the publisher of this work.

The data, facts and description of events forthwith shall be considered as accurate unless the work is deemed to be a work of fiction. In any event, the Publisher is exempt of responsibility for any use of the information contained in the present work on the part of the user. The author and Publisher may not be deemed liable, under any circumstances, for the events resulting from the observance of the advice, tips, techniques and any other contents presented herein.

Given the informational and entertainment nature of the content presented in this work, there is no guarantee as to the quality and validity of the information. As such, the contents of this work are deemed as universal. No use of copyrighted material is used in this work. Any references to other trademarks are done so under fair use and by no means represent an endorsement of such trademarks or their holder.

TABLE OF CONTENTS

Chapter 1: Anxiety and Intimate Relationships 1

What is Relationship Anxiety? 1
How Anxiety Starts in a Relationship 3
Symptoms of Stress and Anxiety in a Relationship ... 8
How Relationship Anxiety Debilitates You 11

Chapter 2: Obstacles in Your Relationship 16

Dynamically Getting to Know your Partner 16
Holes in Your Relationship 20
Self-Deception in a Relationship 24
Discovering Hidden Problems 28
How Pain Can Change a Relationship 31

Chapter 3: Overcoming Obstacles Relationships 35

Adjusting to Your New Reality 35
Filling the Void 37
Stop Blaming Each Other 42
Listen More 47
Get on the Same Page 48
Be Grateful for One Another 53

Chapter 4: Creating a Sense of Security in Your Relationship 60

The Differences Between Thoughts, Emotions, and Actions 60
How to Control Your Feelings 62

Self-Awareness is Key 67

Chapter 5: Developing Self-Awareness 70

Become More Cognizant of Your Feelings 70

Sit with Your Feelings.. 72

Be More Vulnerable.. 74

Talk About Your Feelings... 76

Acknowledge Your Mistakes and Flaws 77

Become More Mindful.. 79

Self-Compassion Can Heal 81

Chapter 6: Beyond Therapy 84

Rediscover What Makes You and Your Partner a Couple 84

Be More Positive... 88

Address Fears of Abandonment 92

Express Understanding.. 96

Use Natural Remedies 99

Rebuild Fragmented Parts of Your Relationships .. 101

Chapter 7: Communication is Key to a Happy Relationship 104

Self-Disclosure 105

Rewards of Self-Disclosure 108

You Can Build Listening Skills 110

Pseudo Listening vs. Real Listening 113

Pseudo Listening Blocks Real Listening................ 118

How to Listen 122

Chapter 8: How to Cultivate Self-Love 129

Practice Generosity 130
Treat Yourself With Kindness 134
Know Who You 136
Honor Parts of Yourself You Hate 138
Learn to Love Flaws 140
Steps to Being in Love with Yourself......142

Chapter 9: Light Up Your Love Life 146

How Anxiety Dulls Relationships............147
How Do I Help My Partner with Anxiety 152

Chapter 10: Keep Your Relationship Flourishing 167

Stay Engaged With Your Partner 168
Complete Projects Together 172
Visible Actions of Love Matter 175
Express Your Feelings 177
Compliment Your Partner........................180
Love in New Ways 183

Chapter 11: Resolve your Differences 186

Be Supportive and More Forgiving 186
Consult with a Professional 197
Fight for Your Relationship 199

CHAPTER 1

Anxiety and Intimate Relationships

What is Relationship Anxiety?

Millions of people have fears about their relationships, and everyone has this anxiety once in a while. When you start to fixate on your doubts all the time, that is when you know that you have a more severe form of relationship anxiety that you need to address if you want to establish healthy relationships or maintain ones you already have. The tips detailed in this book can be helpful for anyone with anxiety or their loved ones.

Relationship anxiety is a feeling of worry, doubt, or other insecurities in a relationship. It is a prominent wedge in many relationships because it makes one or both partners doubt that their relationship is working or that the other person cares for them equally. When you are worried about your relationship, your whole life can crumble as you try to deal with the potential emotional fallout that the end of your relationship can cause. While relationship anxiety can impact any relationship that you have—

familial, platonic, or romantic— this book will focus on the issues related to romantic relationship anxiety and how to address any concerns you may have in intimate relationships.

People who have relationship anxiety may struggle to maintain stable romantic relationships. If you have worries about your romance, it's hard not to become paranoid or insecure. Those insecurities build, and you become unable to handle any doubts you have about your relationship. When you feel like something is wrong with your relationship, your actions may become frantic, which will ruin the emotional and even physical intimacy of your relationship. Additionally, your anxiety could spread to your partner, who will pick up on the signals that you are giving out and may begin to feel equally as frantic as you do. As a result, the foundation of your relationship will erode, and without some serious TLC, it will disintegrate. It is not easy to deal with the changes in a relationship

When you have relationship anxiety, you feel uncertain about the future of your relationship. You think that everything that could go wrong will. Rather than being something that excites you, the future becomes a source of dread because of the changes in your relationship that the future could bring. Your relationship becomes fraught as you cling onto the present and fight a battle that hasn't even happened yet. You become moodier with anxiety, which causes you to overreact and without thinking through the consequences of your actions. For example, if you suspect a partner is cheating merely because of anxiety, you may check your partner's phone for evidence. If your partner catches you checking their phone, the trust you have with them will be broken enough that your relationship becomes fractured.

Relationship anxiety makes it hard to maintain security in a relationship because you frequently feel like your relationship is falling apart, even when it is okay. It is common for people to have relationship anxiety, but when it gets to the point that it takes over your entire relationship, you have a problem that you must address. You cannot allow those stressed feelings you have to fester because if they do, your relationship will never thrive. It will crumble before your eyes, and the less you address your anxiety, the worse it will get until you aren't sure how your relationship can ever be spared from the consequences of your worries.

How Anxiety Starts in a Relationship

Anxiety can begin small, a barely-there whisper, but when you leave it to its own devices, it easily amplifies and becomes a giant monster in your relationship. It can make you go from being an idyllic couple to a terrified one.

When stress begins, you might now notice it. It may just be a tickling in the pit of your stomach or a fluttering of a few butterflies. You may brush it away, thinking that it will vacate your body on its own, but things you pay little attention to have a way of getting louder the more you try to suffocate them and get them to shut up. To deal with worry, you have to give your fears oxygen and face them head-on. Most of all, you have to know how anxiety commonly starts so that you can identify the makings of anxiety within yourself or your partner.

Your insecurities convince you that your partner must be duplicitous. Most relationship anxieties start this way. You think that your partner, for whatever reason, cannot be trusted with your heart. Rational thoughts don't always fuel this insecurity. It would make sense to feel this way if you caught your partner cheating on you, but in the absence of wrongdoing, the feeling that your partner is fooling you can still be profound. No one wants to be a fool, so the idea that we might get tricked can cause us to feel anxious and cast the blame of our feelings onto our partners. When you're insecure, you cannot shut up the narrative that your partner will turn on you, and often, you think that your partner's issues are somehow a reflection on your character.

Little worries build up and become catastrophized when you are worried. It starts with one long night of work, and as your partner works increasingly, you begin to wonder if maybe they are staying away from you. You feel distant from them, and you want to make sense of the distance you feel. Too quickly, you start to think that your partner's absence means that they don't love you anymore. Truthfully, though, they really could just have a lot of work to deal with, or maybe they really are becoming more distant because they have personal issues that they need to work through. You cannot assume that the individual actions of your partner indicate that your relationship is doomed. Looking at the situation with doom and gloom only makes it harder to facilitate healthy communication. Your worry thrives when it takes information out of context and morphs it into something more extensive than it is.

If your partner does something that breaks your trust, it's normal to have worries, but if you want your relationship to work, you cannot hold onto those worries forever. You don't have to stay in the relationship, but if you choose to forgive your partner for the wrongs you have done, you cannot hang those wrong over their heads forever and have a healthy relationship. When your partner breaks your trust, please work with your partner on building it back honestly rather than letting your doubts rule the relationship. It doesn't help you, in the long run, to hold onto your distrust because when you are distrustful, it is hard to build lost trust back.

Changes are typical causes of anxiety. When you experience many changes in your relationship or just in general, you can start to feel ripples rushing through your relationship and threatening the balance that you have. Even exciting new things like the birth of a baby can cause you to question your relationship and wonder if your partner will continue to care for you in the way that you want. It's normal to be apprehensive about change, but don't act like change is a bad omen of relationship woes you will experience. Change is a chance to strengthen your relationship and patch the holes that the past has caused in that relationship.

Past hurts that you have not addressed are some of the biggest causes of present relationship anxiety. These hurts sometimes don't have anything to do with your partner, but they still keep a loop of worry in your head. If your dad died when you were five or your mom left you when you were ten, for instance, you may have a reoccurring loop in your head that you are going to be abandoned or rejected. You feel the insecurities from when you were a child, and they have followed you into your adult relationships. Past hurts aren't going to vanish, but you do need to address their influence on your current partnerships so that you don't get so lost in the past that you ruin your future with someone you love.

Unrealistic expectations can also fuel anxiety. When you don't maintain reasonable expectations, you're always going to be disappointed. No partner can be precisely what you want them to be because they are individuals, and they are not you. You need to accept that whoever your partner is, they are going to have flaws. You won't like every part of your other half, but those things you don't like are parts of that person you cannot change. If those parts make you insecure, do not try to get your partner to change. Instead, address why those aspects of your partner make you feel so insecure. The more you let go of stringent expectations, the easier it will be to exist comfortably in your relationship.

Knowing the roots of relationship anxiety that you have is a crucial way to start curing the worry you feel. You need to know what it is that makes your anxiety begin to spiral. When you know the roots of your fear, your concerns no longer have power over you. You're so much stronger than your anxiety. Accordingly, your relationships don't have to suffer because of any of the fears that linger within you without a rational basis. It takes time to surmount anxiety, but when you do, your relationships will be more profound and healthier than ever before.

Symptoms of Stress and Anxiety in a Relationship

There are some symptoms that you can look out for to figure out if you have anxiety in your relationship. If you have any of these symptoms, the chances are that you have some kind of relationship anxiety. Your partner may also have several of these symptoms because when you have intense fears, your partner tends to become more anxious as well. These are just some of the most common symptoms of anxiety in relationships. Still, no person will experience romantic stress in the same way as others, so it is expected to vary from these typical tendencies. Every person is unique, and your anxiety cannot be reduced to just these symptoms because you and your relationship are so much more than these things. Nevertheless, you'll likely see some commonalities that will help you determine if the feelings you are experiencing are anxiety.

One of the most prominent signs of relationship anxiety is that you need reassurance frequently. When people feel insecure about a relationship, they want frequent verification about themselves or their relationship. You may ask your partner if they like your body several times a week, or you may ask them to remind you of all the things they love about you. You can seek verification in more subtle ways, such as testing them by asking, "Does this dress make my butt look big?" or "Do you like my new cologne?" These questions themselves don't indicate anxiety, but when they are asked with a desired response in mind, you may be seeking reassurance rather than genuinely wanting an opinion. In such cases, you probably are worried that your partner has lost interest or that you aren't good enough for your partner's love.

People with relationship anxiety worry that they matter to their partner. Everyone wants to feel important to their significant other. Still, when you have a constant inner dialogue along the lines of, "I do not matter to them, they love x,y, and z more than they love me," you may be expressing anxious sentiments. There's a difference between enjoying your partner thinking you're important and wanting to prioritize you and *needing* your partner to validate your importance because of self-worth issues. Anxious people often feel lost when they don't get their desired response from their partner, making it hard for them to feel good enough, worsening the anxiety.

Another one of the significant signs of relationship anxiety is that you censor what you say. If you don't feel like you can speak openly because you are worried about what your partner might think or how they might respond, that suggests some severe anxiety in your relationship. You should be open with your partner, and if you can be, there's a reason that you are unable to share parts of yourself, which reflects your anxiety. You may find yourself not saying certain things because you want to maintain the peace and avoid any tension. It is not a healthy way to keep your relationship, and it lets your problems become even more significant than they already were.

When you have relationship anxiety, you may wonder how genuine your relationship is. You start to think that maybe your partner isn't as devoted to you as you are to them. You worry that your partner is deceiving you. Everything starts to become a game of "Is this real, or is this just a façade?" You lose the ability to feel real intimacy because you are so worried that you are being tricked. You grow disconnected from your relationship; the more you wonder if it is real, and as that happens, the relationship starts to fall apart just as you feared that it might, which is a situation that does no one any good.

Breaking up may always be on your mind, even when things are going well in your relationship. You start to think of the end, even before things have started to go downhill. Your doubt and insecurity reap relationship issues that you were worried about, and it reifies them. You bring to life your own anxieties, which makes you think, "My worries were justified," even if they were not. You fear breaking up with your partner, but at the same time, you usher at the end of the relationship with your anxieties because, at the end of the day, fear is debilitating.

How Relationship Anxiety Debilitates You

When you have relationship anxiety, it is bound to debilitate you. There's no escaping the ill-will of your insecurities. They create a cavernous space of doubt and restless energy within you. You struggle to be appeased by even the nicest of your partner's gestures because you have become too cynical and too scared to open your heart and let your partner into your inner world. You stop communicating as much, and when you do speak, you do so shallowly. When you are insecure about your relationship, you also become unsure about yourself, and it becomes harder to accomplish what you set your mind to doing.

Self-sabotaging behavior is typical for people with relationship anxiety. You tend to expect the worst, and then to protect yourself, you engage in actions that sabotage your relationship. For example, when you worry that your partner is distancing from you, you may unconsciously or consciously distance yourself from them to protect yourself. Your brain thinks like this, "If you distance yourself before they can distance from you, you will feel less pain. It is better if you cause the rift than if you let them cause the rift. By distancing myself, I can control my pain." That thought process isn't healthy, but it is normal. When you have anxiety, you want to run away rather than facing your problems, which can result in a self-fulfilling prophecy. By trying to protect yourself from hurt, you create the very situation you worried about. Your partner really does become more distant because they sense the distance you have made to protect yourself.

You stop living in the moment, which leads to the disintegration of your relationship. When you have anxiety, you are prone to rumination, and your head either gets locked into pondering situations that have already happened or that have yet to happen. You become unable to appreciate what is currently happening, and your partner can sense that emotional distance. You miss out on the beneficial moments of the here and now, and you miss so many chances to improve your relationship by now being present. Presence is one of the best ways to help any relationship, and if being present and honest doesn't work, perhaps you need to evaluate further your relationship and what you need from it.

You're not happy when you feel insecure in your relationship. Relationships are one of the most significant parts of life, so when you don't feel content in your relationship, there's an overcast over your entire life. You'll be more cynical at work, with your friends, and even when you're doing the hobbies that make you the most passionate. Your worry may cause mental health issues, such as depression, which can worsen the symptoms you have and make it hard to go about your life with fulfillment. When you become unhappy, something needs to change, and avoiding your anxiety is never the answer. No change will stick if you don't get to the root of your anxiety.

It is hard to move forward in your relationship. You may be wanting to take the next steps in your relationship—marriage, starting a family, buying a home. If you feel anxiety, you may be tentative to move forward with big decisions, even if they would make you content. You start to think, "This relationship is going against the clock, anyway, so it would be foolish to make any big changes." Such a thought process prevents progress, and it makes you feel edgy.

Your partner starts to feel insecure when you are insecure, which only makes your anxiety worse. As you become more anxious, your partner, sensing your anxiety, may think that they have something to worry about as well. You will then absorb some of their nervous energy. Both of you being anxious will make it hard to burst through the worry that you both feel. You'll both be tenser, which will lead to snippiness and less communicative behavior. Anxiety clouds your judgment, and when both people are worrying about a relationship, it can be hard to find solutions that improve each person's mental state.

Relationship anxiety takes up so much of your time that you could spend doing what you love. No matter how much anxiety you have, it takes up time that you could use for productive thoughts. When you spend all your time worrying, you cannot have fun. You lose quality time feeling light and free, which is why it is so important not only to address your anxiety for your relationship but also your personal wellbeing. Anytime that you feel concerned about your relationship, those concerns are going to infiltrate your relationship with yourself. When you address romantic stress, every other relationship you have improves because you can focus on building quality connections instead of fretting.

The more you let anxiety fester, the harder it becomes to combat. Fear doesn't always mean that you are to blame, and often, no one is to blame. It can indicate that your partner is mistreating you, but again, that is less often to be the case. In any case, don't ignore your anxiety. It is trying to tell you something important, and it is trying to protect you. With that in mind, you don't always have to believe what your anxiety is telling you. If your partner is abusing you, by all means, listen to that anxiety, but when that's not the case, be more vigilant about why you feel how you do. If your concern is telling you that you are unlovable and that your partner will leave you without anything to back that notion up, address why you are feeling that way. Then, make efforts to change how you are feeling.

CHAPTER 2

Obstacles in Your Relationship

Dynamically Getting to Know your Partner

Idiosyncrasies are the things you love about others. Thus, learn to embrace those idiosyncratic parts of your partner. If you want to better your relationship, you need to understand your own insecurities and those of your partner. You can't just get to know your partner singlemindedly and only see them in a way that fits the narrative that your anxiety has created. You also can't know your partner based on how they were when you met them ten weeks, ten months, or ten years ago. People are not stagnant beings, which means that you have to keep getting to know your partner, no matter how long you have been with them. Get to know them dynamically, embracing their inconsistencies and changes. People are often oxymorons, and that what makes them so exciting and so fun to get to know. Embrace the eccentricities of your partner because that's the joy of a relationship, and they should accept yours too.

Understand that people are complicated. You're never going to understand your partner entirely. There will always be parts of them that you don't genuinely get, and that's okay. Knowing that you will never know all their experiences and how they function is what allows your relationship to grow infinitely. There's always something you can learn. You won't like everything that you do understand, but you can love a flawed person as a whole. You can learn to accept that people are complicated, which makes relationships complicated too. You never have to apologize for loving someone because often, love is far beyond your control.

Know more than the positive aspects of your partner. Get to know those flaws that you may have been avoiding. The flaws aren't going to make your heart flutter with joy, but some of them you might grow to love, and the others you will learn to accept. If you cannot accept your partner as they are now, you are never going to have a fulfilling relationship. It's acceptable not to agree with the things they do and tell them that they don't agree, but you cannot expect to change them. As lovely as it would be to change people, if the person you're with is not a person like, no combination of the tools in this book will relieve your anxiety because a relationship with someone you cannot enjoy or want to change is never healthy.

Allow constructive criticism. If you don't let your partner make any constructive comments about your role in your relationship, then you are not opening yourself up to working as a team to solve your issues. Verbal abuse and constant criticism are both dreadful, and they are signs of relationships that should end, but being honest and expressing grievances is a vital process of communicating each other's needs. If you want your partner only ever to say good things, your partner will not be frank with you when frankness is required. It can be hard to accept constructive criticism, but giving it and receiving it can make your life so much better.

Understand that your partner will change over time, as will you. You're both going to be different in ten years, and while that idea is terrifying, it doesn't have to be the end of the world. Learn to welcome change. It will be fun to continue to get to know your partner as they change and to let them get to know you. Sharing yourself is one of the most profound experiences that a person can have, and sharing all of yourself over the years is a liberating and heartwarming feeling. It feels good to be known, and it also feels good to know others intimately. Intimacy is so much more than sex. It is allowing every part of yourself to be seen and seeing the details of someone else that are typically hidden. Intimacy is remarkable, especially when you let that intimacy adapt.

Embrace the new parts of your shared life rather than allowing them to paralyze you. When your partner gets a new job, and you have to move two hundred miles away, that change is gigantic. It feels overwhelming, and you question all your lie choices in the face of such a big difference. You start to wonder if you're making the right choice, and you wonder if the change will be the end of everything in your relationship. Stop looking at change like a marker of something going wrong. When things change, it doesn't mean that your relationship is more vulnerable or that something with your partner has gone wrong. All it means is that you have new circumstances and contexts to get to know each other in. How many people say off-handedly, "Oh, wouldn't it be nice to go back to the old days in our relationship and go back to the days of passion." Guess what? Changes are sort of like getting that chance to reget to know each other and revitalize your spark!

Never reduce the issues to what they are on the surface. What is on the surface is not your whole partner, your whole self, or your whole relationship. Remember that people are dynamic. There are multiple levels to every person on this earth, which allows us to be much more than we seem. When you have relationship issues, look beyond what the problems seem to be, and dig into what they really are. Ask yourself how your partner may be feeling beyond their exterior.

If you find yourself looking at your partner as one stagnant thing, you need to change your perception of them before you can do anything else on this journey of anxiety-busting. You wouldn't want to be treated like you were treated ten years ago because you're in a different place now than you were then (hopefully). Thus, you have to allow equal openness and change in your relationship as well. Let your relationship grow, and learn to love the growth because when you do that, you can have a relationship that lasts decades.

Holes in Your Relationship

In every relationship, some holes threaten to get bigger until they consume both you and your partner. Holes in your relationship start small. They are a nuisance, but they do not do much damage. At first, they are barely noticeable, but eventually, you begin to see that the fabric of your relationship is coming apart. These holes can be daunting. You can worry that they are impossible to fill, or you can instead choose to take the time to mend them. Before you can repair the holes, though, you must learn how to spot them. Once you can spot them, you can begin fixing them before they get too bad because the sooner you spot and patch holes in your relationship, the less anxiety you will have.

You may learn that you and your partner may not want the same things from your relationship despite believing that you were on the same page. When people hide many of their feelings from their partner, it is easier to realize that you didn't want the same thing as your partner. You start to understand that your expectations were out of line from theirs, and this understanding causes new issues that pierce holes in your relationship. For example, your partner may be under the impression that you want kids, but you may not expect to have kids. This misunderstanding can cause a rift in your relationship, especially if you don't clear it up.

At times, your morals may clash. No two people will have the exact same morals, which is more profound in certain relationships than it is in others. You might not have the same religion, vote for the same elected officials, or take different stances on important issues. While there's nothing wrong with having unique idea, it can be hard to navigate a relationship in which two people have contrasting views on issues that make their partner passionate. You need to recognize that you cannot expect other people to have the same values as you and try to find respect for the other person's morals. Your morals don't deserve any more respect than your partner's. If you can't get behind that notion, you're probably with someone who is morally incompatible with you, which requires a much larger discussion and intense decisions.

Communication issues are perhaps the most common holes in relationships. People in relationships often don't know how to communicate with each other successfully. They end up yelling rather than having productive conversations that lead to good relational results. When you struggle to communicate, it is usually because you are not being open to what one another is saying. You assume that you know the points they want to get across without actually taking the time to listen. It is hard to be a good communicator, but you need to make efforts to be more open to what your partner is saying and allow calm speech before you both take to yelling. By simply being more openminded, you can take a significant step forward in your communication. Additionally, you cannot censor yourself just to keep the peace because that censorship will lead to unaddressed feelings getting worse.

You may become bitter about things that you never really got over in your relationship. Sometimes, you say, "It's fine. I don't mind," when, in reality, you do mind. This use of language is always harmful. There's nothing wrong with making concessions and sacrifices, but you should be upfront when you do care. You should say, "Doing this is not what I want, but I am going to learn to accept this course of action because it's what you want, and I value your happiness and do not think this specific thing is worth a big argument." Explaining yourself shouldn't be seen as starting a fight or making trouble where you don't need to make it. Healthy relationships require honesty and communication of how you are feeling. Make sure that your partner is open to hearing what you have to say, and ensure that you are open to hearing what your partner has to say at well. Relationships are a two-way street, so don't try to hide when you're upset. You don't have to fly off the handle and start yelling that you are upset, but find ways to express your honest feelings, even if those feelings aren't convenient.

Many couples lose track of passion over time. They become so used to the typical activities of being in a relationship that they lose track of what made them fall in love in the first place. The spark dies, and with it, so can a person's confidence in the relationship. The passion you have in a relationship doesn't have to be the same five years in versus ten years into the relationship. Still, passion should exist in some manner to keep the relationship secure and ensure that each person feels like the relationship is giving them what they need. Don't just have passion, but express it. Your partner needs to see that you are still passionate, and you need to see it from them as well.

Material issues such as money problems can cause additional holes in healthy relationships. When you are struggling to make ends meet, it is easy to blame each other for your situation and let bitterness settle. It is easier to address the grievance you have against your partner than to deal with the overwhelming implications of a bad financial situation. Money is one of the most common aspects of life that cause couples to fight, which is why it is extra essential that you pay attention to your financial worries and ensure that your money anxiety doesn't turn into romantic stress.

Illnesses are sometimes unavoidable, but they can also be significant points of fear among couples. If you or your partner has been diagnosed with a severe or life-changing illness, it can heavily influence your relationship. Illnesses cause a myriad of unwanted issues that can cause a couple to fight because of all the fear and worry they have related to the disease. It can also add responsibility to one of the partner's loads, which naturally causes extra stress and uncertain dynamics between partners. Health conditions are no one's fault, and you cannot prevent them, but you can prevent them from ruining your relationship.

These issues are just some of the most common problems that couples face. There's a long list of other holes in your relationship that may cause you to struggle. Acknowledge the main struggles that you have to endure and be ready to make considerable changes to address the gaps life has left in your relationship. Some of these gaps are beyond your control, but no matter what the cause, you can mend the holes, and you can learn to respond as well as you can to hardships. The strength of a relationship is in how you react to life's challenges as a team. If you work together and stop ignoring the holes in your relationship, you can mend them before they become too ginormous.

Self-Deception in a Relationship

Another huge factor that exacerbates relationship issues is people fooling themselves. When you have problems in a relationship, you don't want to admit your own responsibility or even admit that a problem exists at all. As anxiety is sharp in your core and flutters in your stomach, you try to cast blame on other areas of your life. You ignore the fear, attributing it to something less intense. In the process, you start to fool yourself, and you lose track of the issue in a web of your own self-deception. You need to be honest with yourself because if you cannot be honest with yourself, you will never have the tools to improve your relationship anxiety.

When you have anxiety, it can be hard to tell if your fears are genuine or merely anxious. Anxiety causes you to lose track of the root of your fears, and they all swirl together, causing chaos in your brain. Some fears are genuine and stem from past challenging experiences that taught you the dangers of the world. For example, you may know that it is dangerous to grab a bee because it will sting you. That fear of holding a bee is warranted, but other fears such as not wanting to sit outside because a bee might be out there is not justified. Not all your worries are equally rational, but they can all feel the same, which is why you need to take the time to sort through what is anxiety and what is a reasonable fear.

People who have anxiety often tend to blame their partner without looking at their own responsibility in the problems in the relationship. It's easy to say, " I give and I give, and I give, but my partner just never gives back to me. They make my life so hard." Sometimes, there is a relationship imbalance, and that needs to be remedied, but other times, couples who have this mentality are acknowledging all of what their partner doesn't do and none of what they do do. Just one person has no relationship, so you can't avoid being part of the problem. Unless your partner is abusive, you likely have a role in the dysfunction.

Tackle the narrative you have about your relationship and determine if you are entirely honest with yourself. Everyone has narratives about their lives, and in many ways, these narratives are fictional. They have seeds of truth, but they can never represent the full truth because our perspectives limit us. You see one small part of the world, and you create a perception of your relationship, and this isn't always the same perception that your partner sees. Try to look beyond your limited first-person narrative and explore how your partner may be viewing your relationship. Understand that your partner has a different perspective, and that perspective can help you reduce your self-deception. Your partner will not always agree about what is happening in your relationship, which doesn't mean that they are lying. They merely see things differently, and you need to see how they are seeing. By doing this, you can emerge from your self-deception just a little bit.

Be more mindful of your relationship. Any good relationship requires you to be present. Don't let past actions of your partner become overly weighted in your judgment about them in the present. Use present information and feelings to most influence your current perception. When you can do that, you can be more honest with yourself about what is bothering you and what you need to change to feel more secure in your relationship. Be mindful by reminding yourself to be present and to analyze your current situation. Mindfulness takes practice, but in no time, you can use it to promote honesty with yourself and to eradicate self-deception as much as possible.

Learn the parts of yourself that you struggle to be honest about, which are usually things that bring you shame or self-doubt. There are undoubtedly parts of yourself that you don't typically appreciate. Maybe you force yourself to laugh differently because you hate your usual laugh. Such behavior is not being honest about yourself. It is trying to force yourself to fit a mold that you don't fit. You need to embrace yourself rather than alienating your traits from yourself.

If you are deceiving yourself, you are never going to work through your problems, so stop trying to convince yourself that your situation is less complicated than it is. Stop blaming other areas of your life. Allow yourself to be honest about the causes of your relationship anxiety. If you aren't willing to be honest about that, you might as well close this book right now because you'll never feel free of anxiety until you stop trying to fool yourself. Help your partner work through their self-deception as well to ensure you are both ready to go forward.

Discovering Hidden Problems

You need to uncover the issues that either you or your partner have kept hidden. Because of relationship holes and self-deception, it is expected that some hidden problems will develop. These issues fly under the radar and that both partners in a relationship don't initially recognize as a problem. You can find these problems by learning to be more transparent with your concerns and digging into parts of your relationship that you have neglected as you avoided addressing your festering anxiety. You need to do a deep dive into your relationship and your partner, even if you think you know them well.

Communicate issues that you have kept from your partner. The first step to discovering problems that you didn't know existed is confiding in your partner problems that you have that you never told them, and give them the chance to talk about what they have kept hidden as well. Allow them to be part of your life, and show them that you're open to listening to whatever they have to say. You should not go into this process if you are going to be judgmental. Be as openminded as you can so that you both feel safe to whatever it is that you need to discuss.

Show your partner that you are willing to be openminded to whatever they have to say. Don't just be openminded, but express that you are eager to listen to them, even if they have something hard to tell you. Explain to them that you'd prefer honesty and to clearly know where you both stand. Even if it gets hard to keep your mouth shut, do so to prove that you are not going to cut in before they have told you what they need to say. Thinking you are open is different than showing that you are open, so find ways to do both. By doing that, you will allow more conversations between you and your partner so that less information will stay hidden in the future, and you both can be highly communicative.

Hold your partner accountable for communication just as you hold yourself accountable. If your partner isn't doing their part in helping you unravel the bundled up issues of your relationship, you need to be firm with them and explain that you both have to participate if you want to make a difference in your relationship. If your partner isn't even willing to try and be cooperative in this process, you have much bigger issues than just relationship anxiety. You may need to seek additional professional assistance from a professional if your partner is unwilling to use the methods detailed in this book.

Know that problems are often much more profound than they seem. Little issues like not taking out the trash don't seem like they are that important, but they can represent broader issues and feelings that one or both of the partners in a relationship have. For example, one couple, Warren and Sherri, would always bicker. Sherri was especially upset about their situation. She hated how Warren would never rinse out his dish, and it seems like such a small issue, but it comes down to Sherri feeling disrespected. Back when he was much younger, Warren complained about how disrespectful it was when his roommates didn't rinse their dishes. Thus, Sherri felt that Warren didn't respect her when he didn't rinse his dish. Warren never realized Sherri felt that way until she finally confessed it to him, and he realized that he was acting in a way that sent the wrong message. Through little problems like that, Sherri and Warren could patch up their relationship and are stronger than ever.

Hidden problems are often linked with shame. Couples may feel embarrassed about their issues, which makes them even harder to address. A woman, for example, maybe embarrassed to talk to her husband about topics related to menopause or other womanly experiences that most men have not gone through. Some of the silence in relationships is fueled by cultural taboos and embarrassment over normal human functions. It may be challenging, but you need to cut through your shame and realize that whatever issues you have shouldn't be too awkward to discuss with your partner.

Once you have found hidden problems, you have new consciousness of issues you otherwise didn't address. Covert issues have a way of growing when you don't address them, so be sure that you and your partner start to do some digging to see what is genuinely causing issues in your relationship. What you find may surprise you, but when you find the roots of your problems, you can start to combat them, and in the process, you can ease the anxiety you feel about your relationship. You'll feel much better when you establish more honesty in your relationship.

How Pain Can Change a Relationship

Pain is a huge influencer in how you feel overall and how you feel in your relationship. Pain can go much beyond physical pain, and it can include emotional or even spiritual pain. When one or both partners are hurting in your relationship, there are bound to be shifts in how you behave and what you need. Pain requires change, but many couples in relationships fail to bring the necessary change as the pain occurs. They think that they can continue as they usually would, but that won't allow for the continued strength that all relationships need. The pain will erode the unchanged relationship and do more harm than good. Pain makes people see life differently, and it makes them see their relationships in a new light too, so embrace the newness rather than trying to avoid it.

Physical pain can cause friction in relationships. Whatever it is that physically hurts can make you less able to do the tasks you would typically do. As a result, the dynamic between you and your partner can change. Research has shown that people with chronic pain often have greater levels of pain in the morning, and when this happens, they have more problems with their relationships when it becomes night. This information shows how pain wears a person down and makes them feel like a shell of who they once were. Pain makes it hard to have the skills and energy required to balance a relationship. When you are in pain, you aren't always yourself, and partners don't know how to help without being too pushy.

One couple, Roger and Jay, were altered by Roger's arthritis. At the young age of thirty-four, Roger began to experience increased pain in his joints. As his condition wore on, he would struggle to do tasks such as washing dishes, which was one of his regular household chores. Because of Roger's physical limitations, the couple had to redistribute their duties and find new ways to run their household. As they learned to deal with Roger's pain rather than pushing through it, their relationship became more comfortable, and their anxieties lessened.

Additionally, emotional pain can also cause extensive rifts in relationships that worsen anxiety. Physical pain is only one kind of pain, and it isn't always the most harmful for a relationship. If someone who is depressed, anxious, or otherwise mentally ill is in a relationship, there are unique challenges that a couple facing those illnesses will have to handle and adjust accordingly. Even if no one is mentally ill, average emotional ups and downs have consequences and can lead to emotional imbalance and confusion in a relationship. Emotional pain is one of the most significant factors to consider if you have relationship anxiety, and it and physical pain can be linked. When you or your partner have physical discomfort, you may also have emotional distress because of the challenges associated with the physical trauma.

If you are responsible for caring for your partner, that responsibility can add even more strain on a relationship already riddled with hardship. Caretakers can often be stretched thin, and those who are being cared for may feel guilty for their partner's burden. Thus, the dynamics of the relationship change, and both partners feel uncertain in their roles. Couples may not know how to behave around each other anymore, or they may struggle to understand how to relate in ways not associated with the illness or pain that one or both of them are experiencing. Pain and disease are often unexpected, which means couples are frequently thrown into situations that they weren't physically or mentally ready to deal with, promoting anxiety in their relationship.

As you get older, you often experience additional pain or new physical limitations that make it hard to manage your lifestyle. Old age is hard for many people to face, and even relationships that are decades old can struggle from the changes that come with getting older. You may be unable to do the things together that you usually would have when you were younger, which means that you'll have to find new ways to connect and spend time with one another.

Know that sometimes you will have to adjust to the pain and learn new ways to relate to the other person in your relationship. When you have pain, you need to remain conscious of how that pain impacts your relationship or how your partner's pain influences you. There's no perfect way to deal with pain in a relationship, but if you become more aware of its role in your relationship, you can avoid some of the consequences that may result from the pain you or your partner feels. It takes time to learn how to deal with pain or illness, but it is not an impossible feat.

CHAPTER 3

Overcoming Obstacles Relationships

Adjusting to Your New Reality

When you have determined what your main relationship obstacles are, you can then begin addressing those issues. Your relationship will start to develop in a new reality. Things that you saw in a certain way before, you will see in news ways. Your newfound understanding of your relationship will help you add new context to old misunderstandings that confounded both you and your partner and make you anxious. Your anxiety cannot destroy your relationship if you fight against it, so fight those worried thoughts and learn that they are not always right.

Keep being honest with yourself. Honesty is not just a one-time thing that you can practice once and be done with. It is a practice that you will have to continue throughout your relationship, especially during rough patches. You don't have to share everything with your partner. Sometimes, there are specific thoughts that you need to process alone, but lying is not appropriate. If you don't want to share, you can say something like, "I'm still processing these thoughts that I am having, so it's nothing personal, but I need to figure out some stuff in my head before I share." This excuse is not a catchall excuse. When your partner should know something for their safety or someone else's safety, you need to tell them, but when it is something personal to you, you can hold back for a little while. Staying too distant will hurt your relationship, so be careful about how much you keep to yourself.

Accept that things are different than they were, but that fact doesn't have to be a horrendous part of life. Your new normal is an opportunity for both your relationship to grow but also yourself. When you allow change, you can grow into yourself and explore other passions you have otherwise denied yourself. You discover parts of yourself outside your relationship, and when that happens, you feel more secure in your relationship because your sense of self is influenced by more than who you are dating or who you married! You realize that while your relationship is part of you, it is not all of you.

Know that you cannot control what will happen. Sometimes, relationships have to end. Don't get so fixated on the fact that your relationship might end that you cannot see the ways it is struggling right now. Don't avoid your issues just because you say, "Oh, the relationship is bound to end anyone." When you have that attitude, you take responsibility away from yourself, and you put it on fate. You have the power to influence your relationship's future, so use that power in ways that benefit you rather than hurt you!

Believe that there is hope for your anxiety to be less than it is right now. There is hope for the future. No matter how much anxiety you have right now, it can get better if you practice the techniques discussed in this book. You may feel like you can never be secure in a relationship, but everyone can have relationship security with time and work. Anxiety is just a feeling, which means that while it can influence you heavily, it cannot control you. If you want your relationship to work, tell anxiety that it is not the one running the show. You and your partner are the ones running the show.

Filling the Void

When there are holes in your relationship, you need to fill them, and you need to fill the gaps withing yourself. When there are any gaps in your life, there is room for bad influences to crawl in. The bad influences weaken the fibers of your relationship, and they make it hard to repair the damage that has been done by other forces. In many cases, bad influences make more gaps because they don't actually solve your problem. They don't make you feel more complete, more alive, or less anxious. The inappropriate void fillers such as – mind-altering substances, excessive shopping, and yelling – only serve to make you and your relationship feel emptier. You'll only ever crave more just to get some sense of being filled.

Instill activities that make you feel like a whole person into your life. You need to feel like you are worthwhile as a person independent of your relationship status, as mentioned previously. When you choose new activities, or you revive old ones, you learn about yourself, and your discover parts of yourself that you've probably kept hidden from the surface. When activities make you feel good without being destructive, self-destructive, or compulsive, then they are suitable activities to do more of so that you never feel like half a person just because you are one half of your relationship. Never deny yourself harmless activities that give you real joy.

Try new activities with your partner. Spending more quality time with your partner is a vital step in easing relationship anxiety. You shouldn't just invest in activities that make you feel alive, but you should also invest in ones that you can share with your partner because by sharing an activity, you are opening yourselves up to one another. Maybe try an activity that your partner loves, but you usually dislike and expect your partner to do the same for you. I'm not saying to force yourself to do something that you hate, but expand your comfort zone and give a little to your partner while expecting them to give as well. Alternatively, you can try activities that neither you nor your partner has much experience doing.

By doing this, you're starting something new with someone you love, which is a great bonding activity that reduces anxiety.

Find passion in your relationship, no matter how old it is. You are never too old to have passion. Your passion doesn't have to be the same as it was when you were younger, but it should exist. Little aspects of a relationship can allow sparks to fly and revive the enthusiasm that you share for each other. Passion can be sexual, but it certainly doesn't have to be. It can also be found in activities like sharing a nice meal or going away on a trip together. It can be renewing your vows or spending time with your children. Anything that makes you feel brighter and more inspired by one another can invoke passion.

Force yourself to be honest, even if it hurts and even if it ends the relationship. If you get nothing else from this book, I want you to absorb this recurring theme: truth hurts sometimes, but it is the best option. Truth isn't just a matter of confessing wrongs. It includes candor, the incredible act of being open, and it includes vulnerability, which refers to intimate openness. Being more genuine makes your relationship feel less hollow, and you can accomplish honesty in so many ways. Don't limit how you will be honest. Even just saying "You look nice" to your partner when you think it is a suitable way of being honest. The bottom line is that honesty is about sharing yourself, even when doing so doesn't come naturally.

Put less emphasis on outside pressures or find ways to reduce exterior forces. Be mindful of the internal workings of your relationship so that the external pressures cannot influence you as much. If you have robust internal devices, you can fight any outside forces that threaten your relationship. One couple, Mary and Al, had this exact issue. Al was diagnosed with cancer, and while it was treatable, it caused strain in his relationship with Mary. They began strengthening their inner selves, and so when the doctors gave the bad news that Al's cancer had advanced, they were better able to deal with the crippling outside forces that threatened the security of their relationship.

Heal old wounds. If you're angry at your partner for something that happened ten years ago, no matter how much you say you're over it, you're not over it. If your mom died when you were twelve, making you afraid of abandonment and that fear impacts your relationship, you have internal work to do. None of your old wounds should be so strong that they can destroy your relationship, but when old wounds aren't giving the time and resources to heal, they don't get better, and you can never have peace in your relationship. You will always fear the what-ifs until you learn to face them. Working through your issues feels draining, but it will revitalize you in the long run.

Make more positive meaning. Your relationship probably means a lot to you in a myriad of ways, so give the positive parts a higher value. Take the information you have about your relationship and look at it in a new way that emphasizes the vital areas rather than the wrong areas that only leave you feeling anxious. Give your relationship a new purpose and discover the positive ways it impacts you right now. You get to decide the meaning of your relationship, so make it a good purpose if you want to feel better. When you can make more positive meaning in your life, you tell anxiety that it cannot change what your relationship means to you.

Address your pains and your partner's pains. It's time to stop avoiding all the hurts you have. Even the little hurts that you have need to become a part of the discussion. Some pains won't be healed. They will linger, and they will always hurt, but that doesn't mean you should give up on your relationship. Allow the pain to be part of you, but do not allow it to define you or your relationship. You are multi-faceted, and pain is just one facet. It is not your personality or your worth; it is merely a part of being alive. Stop trying to deny or downplay your pain and acknowledge it for what it is.

When you find ways to fill the holes you have, it's easier to have a healthy relationship. The holes you have in your relationship have plenty of acceptable fillers that won't add to your anxiety. When you tend to the issues of your relationship with care and patience, you find much better results than when you treat your issues with haste. Take your time, and allow the problems to be raw for a while rather than hoping for them to go away instantly.

Stop Blaming Each Other

Too often, couples blame each other for relationship woes, and this leads to distrust and increased levels of anxiety. Blaming one another hasn't helped you so far, so it's unlikely that it ever will. When you blame your partner, you take responsibility away from yourself. While sometimes your partner will have more fault in an issue, blame is endless. It keeps going with no constructive feedback, so it never creates a conversation that leads to emotional development. Blame always causes more anxiety because it spirals and continues in a degrading cycle. It jades you and makes you wonder if your relationship is worth the fight.

The first way to stop blaming your partner is to be more compassionate. Learn that you cannot expect them to be perfect, or you will be unhappy. Your partner will make mistakes and do things that you disagree with, but you should be more understanding of your partner's flaws rather than blaming your partner's flaws for every issue that you have. Your deficiencies contribute to your relationship woes too, and by not being compassionate to your partner, you lose sight of all your partner's finer qualities, the ones that will help you improve your situation. A little understanding goes a long way in establishing relationship security.

Stop trying to deflect your anxiety. People tend to project their fears onto other things. Thus, you may be projecting your worries onto inappropriate sources such as your partner. If you're afraid of your partner cheating, and your partner has never cheated, then saying, "But my partner is so __, so they must cheat," is deflecting your anxiety onto your partner. You're taking the responsibility of your anxiety away from yourself by stating that some inherent quality causes it in your partner. Deflection is natural, but you need to catch yourself in the act to understand your anxiety for what it is.

Accountability and blame are two different entities. It's one thing to hold your partner accountable for the things they do that are wrong, and it's another thing altogether to blame them for issues that they had no fault in. When you hold someone accountable, you force them to be responsible for their action, but blame doesn't require responsibility. It is just an admittance of fault, whether that fault is valid or not. If your partner cheats on you, you should hold them accountable, but if you think your partner might cheat, then you shouldn't blame them for your anxiety because they haven't done anything wrong, so they cannot be held accountable. Blame doesn't require guilt, but accountability can.

Know that you are both responsible for the outcomes of your relationship. As one half of the relationship, you are responsible for what occurs in your relationship and how you deal with those happenings. When your partner wrongs you, you get to decide based on the context of your relationship how to go forward, but your partner also has a say in how you proceed. If someone doesn't have a say in the outcomes of a relationship, then you aren't going to move forward with a firm footing and could sabotage your chances of improving yourselves as a couple and individuals.

Learn to catch when your partner is unfairly blaming you. Hold your partner accountable for times when they don't rightly blame you because you don't deserve blame for concerns that you can't control or aren't your fault. When your partner unfairly blames you, do not become hostile. Calmly explain how your partner is unjust with you because calm language will make your partner more likely to listen to what you are saying without becoming defensive. Always remember that people don' react logically, especially to criticism, so don't expect that having the necessary conversations will always be easy. With time and practice, you and your partner should master the skills to be honest with each other more easily.

You also need to know when your partner is rightly pointing out your faults. Be able to admit, "Yeah, I do that, and it is wrong, but I want to do better moving forward." Listen to what your partner is saying because they're trying to show you what they need from you for the relationship to work. You are not always in the right and know when you're not in the right. Don't let your partner degrade you and always tell you that you are wrong, but be honest with yourself and your partner about your issues and your role in your relationship's problems. It can be hard to own up to your faults, but when you do, a weight will be lifted from your shoulders.

Accept your flaws. Don't drive yourself crazy over things that you don't like about yourself. It's useless to expect to be the perfect partner, and it would be boring to be the ideal partner, anyway. If you don't even accept your flaws, you can't expect that your partner will either. You need to admit to yourself that you are only human, which means that you don't always get it all right and that you have certain traits that make you hard to deal with and even irrational at times. Your imperfection doesn't take away from your worth as a person. You are still just as worthy, and when you accept your flaws, you can learn to lessen their impact on your relationship.

Share your perspective but be open to your partner's perspective too. It's good to be candid with your partner, but don't get into the habit of only sharing and not listening. Your view is critical, but don't get so fixated on it that you become rigid and refuse to see things from your partner's perspective. Your partner needs to know that you are willing to accept their view, even if you do not love it, and sometimes, you will have to meet them halfway. It can never be your way or the highway because if it is, your relationship will become insecure.

Be constructive rather than destructive. When you're honest about each other's faults, you don't want to tear down your partner, and they shouldn' tear you down either. The point of honesty is to build each other up. Thus, you shouldn't make comments to make your partner feel bad or have no potential to build your relationship. Your comments should always be constructive. Tell your partner what you have a problem with and tell them what would make that issue better for you. When you give wrongs without giving any ways to improve those wrongs, you are blaming rather than being constructive.

When your partner does blame you, know that while your partner's words are directed at you, those words are not essentially about you. Blame comes from a place of personal insecurity, and while that does not make it appropriate, it does show that blame reflects more on the person who is blaming than on the person who is being blamed. Blame, when it happens, can highlight the insecurities in your relationship and show what you need to address first. You can take that blame and turn it into constructive information that will help you both address what is bothering you within your romance.

It's okay to make mistakes in a relationship, but casting blame often does more harm than good. When you blame someone else, you take no responsibility for yourself, and you close your mind to the multi-faceted explanations that most commonly cause relationship woes. It usually isn't just one thing or person who cracks the foundation of a relationship. More often, several factors contribute to cause romantic destruction, which leads to romantic anxiety. Thus, you should be open to all the facets that influence your relationship and seek to build yourselves back up using all the information you have gathered.

Listen More

Listening, a skill that is detailed throughout this book, is one of the most beneficial ways to overcome the obstacles of your relationship because good listening facilitates good communication. If you're not listening to your partner, you're letting your doubts overwhelm your perception of your relationship. You're becoming intransigent, an unmovable force who is unwilling to take the steps needed to improve your anxiety. The more you get stuck in your anxiety, the harder it is to be flexible and open to what your partner is saying. When you don't listen, your partner stops talking, thinking you don't care what they have to say anyway.

When you listen, do not make assumptions. You cannot know what your partner is going to say before you hear their full explanation. Do not act like you know exactly what they mean one sentence into explantation. You need to hear your partner out, or else you aren't genuinely listening, and you are only acting like you are listening, which is not helpful. Avoid judgments based on preconceptions of the situation because until you fully hear what your partner has to say, you cannot presume to understand.

Listen to what your partner isn't saying. You can observe emotions when someone else speaks, and even if your partner isn't explicit with every detail, you can learn a lot from what they are saying and how they are saying it. Listen between the words just as you would read between the lines. When you listen, you are less judgmental and more open to seeing reason rather than being driven by anxiety. Good listeners have better relationships, and they don't have to be as anxious.

Get on the Same Page

You and your partner need to be a team if you want to reduce the stress you have in your relationship. These suggestions should all be mutual. Relationships need balance, which entails both partners investing time, energy, and care into the relationship.

Have regular discussions about what you both want. Update each other on your dreams, ambitions, and goals. When you keep each other updated, your hopes will never get lost under the longings of your partner. When you're honest about what you expect and what you want the future to look like, there is less room for dissonance, and you will not feel stifled in the relationship. Some relationships can be stifling. They make you feel you must sacrifice your dreams for your partner's goals. No one should feel like that. In a healthy relationship, both parties will feel they have the space they need to grow into their best self.

Ask, don't demand. You don't have the right to tell your partner what they should do, but you can ask them to do something. Don't expect that they will always oblige to your wishes, but you should expect that they will at least listen to what you want. In return, you have to listen to what they want as well. Demands are not an excellent emotional currency in a relationship, but when you ask, you give your partner freedom while still expressing your wants. Orders are a sign of miscommunication in a relationship while asking represents relationship vulnerability.

Logic isn't always the driving force behind what you or your partner is thinking, so learn to be in tune with the emotional elements of humanity. Your partner is not always going to look at a situation through a logical lens. What they say and what they are often going to be driven by emotions. You are the same way. Thus, in a relationship, you have to leave room for the typical emotional responses people face.

Don't expect things to be the same each year. Just because you've had a vacation every year for three years doesn't mean that your partner plans on going on holiday each year for the rest of your life. Expectations can often lead to disappointments, so you need to openminded and realize that your partner may not even realize your expectations. When they fail to meet those expectations, they won't realize that they are hurting you. Some expectations are enforceable like expectations that your partner will respect you, won't hurt you, and be faithful to you. Expectations like expecting flowers for your birthday can lead to issues when they aren't properly communicated.

Remember that your experiences will be relative to your circumstances. Your experiences matter in context because not getting the vacation you wanted because your partner wasted money on something you didn't agree on isn't the same as the vacation not being feasible with your new budget. What seems right at one point in time won't necessarily seem right at another time. For example, if you do go on vacation every year, that experience may not be as practical if you have three kids and a whole lot less money. Expectations and the experiences you have will shift as you go through your relationship and have new concerns to consider.

If your partner values something, learn to respect whatever it is, even if you don't believe in it. If you cannot respect your partner's values, you might be too different or too stubborn to bridge the gaps in your relationship. You don't have to believe in everything that your partner believes in, but you need to be able to say, "I don't agree with you, but I respect your decision to look at things that way." When you have strong feelings about matters such as religion or politics, it can be hard to get on the same page as your partner, but as long as you know where you both stand on matters and accept that, you can have a secure relationship.

Be more flexible. Relationships require flexibility. If your partner has sensitivities, be mindful of their potential fears just as you want them to be aware of yours. Allow yourself to be open to change to make things work. Adapt to what each day brings you, and be mindful that you'll never stop having to adjust and tweak your relationship. Just like you take your car in for regular maintenance, your relationship requires regular maintenance too.

Learn how your partner expresses their feelings and insist they learn these things about you too. When your partner is angry, they may cry, or when they are sad, they may yell. Sometimes what people are really feeling doesn't match their expression of that feeling. Accordingly, you need to learn your partner's emotional clues and be more mindful of their reactions to stressful situations. When you accomplish that task, you can understand your partner better and defuse difficult situations with more adeptness.

You cannot change your partner, so don't try. Some people look for fixer-uppers when they enter a relationship, but humans aren't houses that you can flip and sell for double the price or purchase. Romance isn't a commodity or a financial investment, so you cannot expect to get more out. You can improve your relationship and invest effort into the relationship, but you can't turn the person you're with into a better person or one closer to your desired specifications. Your goal should be to bring out the best of your partner and to help them be their best selves, but you're in your relationship for the wrong reasons if you think you can shift your partner's core personality.

Don't let other people tell you how your relationship should look. While good advice can be helpful, you don't have to let anyone define what your relationship should look like (not even this book can represent your relationship fully). You and your partner are the ones who get to decide how you define your relationship, and society nor the people in it should force you to experience romance in any particular way.

Learn to meet each other halfway. Neither you have to give up everything, but something's got to give. You can't both maintain your life as it is while merging your lives. If you can't make compromises, you'll live separate lives, which is fine if that's what you want to do, but living separate lives isn't much of a romantic relationship. Assert what you want in your relationship, but be open to adjusting your lifestyle and incorporating elements of your parter's lifestyle. Both of you will be happier when you allow flexibility and gradually find a middle ground.

Believe in your partner, even when it is hard. Never assume the worst. When you are faced with doubts, you can investigate them, but don't automatically villainize your partner. Getting on the same page allows you to know your partner better, and it will enable you to merge your lives while still having your individuality and sense of self. Two individuals will always struggle to reconcile one another's life, but that is the joy of being a couple and letting another person into your innermost world.

Be Grateful for One Another

Studies show that people who use gratitude tend to have better heart health, are mentally clearer, and live longer. These impacts can then translate into making your relationship healthier too. Additional research has shown that people who use gratitude in their relationships have longer and stronger relationships. When you are grateful for your current relationship and your past experiences, you are in a better, more tranquil mindset that allows you to have your best relationship yet.

Learn to be thankful, not resentful. When you have the urge to be bitter, think about what you are lucky to have and all the good aspects of your relationship instead. Take the resentment you feel and turn it into thankfulness. Focus on your blessings because when you focus on your gifts, you change your outlook, and you become more positive. When you are resentful, you accomplish nothing, but when you make an effort to be thankful, you see the world as more precious, and you see your relationship that way too. The more grateful you become for your relationship, the easier it will be to combat your anxiety.

Nice gestures aren't just for special occasions. While going out to a nice dinner seems like something you only do on anniversaries or birthdays, it shouldn't be. Doing nice things with your partner should be a regular occurrence. You don't have to spend a lot of money to do nice things, but simply having a regular night out or treating your partner to flowers can be a nice gesture that shows you are grateful to have them in your life. When you see something they like at the store, pick it up even if it wasn't on the grocery list. Take out the trash when it isn't your turn. Give them a little note expressing your love. These acts can seem sappy or silly, but they aren't. They are acts that show you care, which will strengthen your relationship and make you feel better about where you stand in your romance.

Make some sacrifices. In every relationship, both partners have to make sacrifices. Don't give up on things that make you happy or keep you physically or mentally well, but when you can, give a little to your partner. When you want to go to the zoo with the kids, but your partner wants to go to the aquarium, compromise, and say, "We can go to the aquarium some other time." When you're in a relationship, you cannot always get your way, and allowing one another to have the things that mean the most to each of you is one of the best ways you can ensure that you are both happy and healthy in your relationship. Sacrifices can be small, and sometimes they might be big, but neither person in the relationship should be a martyr. Neither of you should have to give up big pieces of yourself just to appease the other.

Enjoy your time together. When you are together, let yourself have fun. Don't get caught up thinking about everything else that you could be doing. If you're watching a TV show together, engage in the show. Don't let your mind wander to work call you have the next morning or what you're going to make for dinner. Even if the activity isn't your first choice, find enjoyment because you're spending time with someone you love. My dad is a big baseball fan, and I've never enjoyed the sport myself, but I'll go to games with him because I know he enjoys it. I have fun going to the games. Still, I wouldn't say I like baseball itself, but I enjoy sitting in the stands with my dad and enjoying the camaraderie of the moment. The same dynamic should be true of romantic relationships. It's thrilling to see a smile on another person's face and be part of that moment.

Be tactile! Touching your partner is one way to ground yourself and remind yourself to be thankful. A hug, a kiss, or even just a gentle hand on the arm can be reassuring and facilitate a connection between you and your partner.

Let the light of your love shine through your eyes. Your partner will be reassured by the warm energies that you give off. As a result, those energies will be returned to you, which will make you feel comforted in your relationship. Generally, when there is relationship insecurity, that insecurity spreads to both partners, so a sense of security can go a long way.

Think of your relationship as a precious gift. It is a present from the universe that you must cherish, and you have to care for it. A relationship requires upkeep, but even with all the work, you are lucky to have it. Not everyone is so fortunate, so you have to keep your gift sparkly and working smoothly.

Laugh more with your partner. Laughter is really one of the best medicines that you can have in life. The more you laugh with someone, the deeper your connection becomes. Laughter is linked to reduced stress and anxiety, so simple actions like watching a comedy special together or sharing inside jokes can release some of the tension between you and your partner and remind you how fortunate you are to have them.

When you have anxiety, think of the positive qualities of your relationship. Let those qualities dull the anxious thoughts that you have. Instead of thinking, "They might leave me," think, "They are with me right now." Remind yourself of the present moment by reminding yourself how lucky you are to have your relationship. Remind yourself that, "I don't know what the future holds, but I am enjoying right now, and I am lucky to have my partner, who cares for me in ways that make me so blessed." Think about the here and now of your relationship and let those thoughts overwrite the anxious thoughts.

Remind yourself of everything that your partner has done for you. If you're in a relationship worth anything, your partner has probably done several things to help you over your time together. Don't forget the kindnesses your partner has done on to you because not all partners do that. You forget that little things like making you coffee in the morning are acts are love. You come to expect them rather than acknowledging them as daily gifts. Those daily gifts are not ones that you can afford to forget. Your partner surely does small things that prove that there's still love between you. Take time to remember those little things.

Honor your past partnerships that have failed, and acknowledge the lessons that they have taught you. Being grateful for past relationships helps you move on from them. When you honor your past, you can let go of old hurts and learn to live in the present. Your old relationships aren't parts of you that you have to forget just because you're in a new relationship. You can embrace that those old relationships were once a significant part of your life without them being significant presently. Old relationships never go away, so be sure to recognize them for the gifts and pain they gave you, and know that your new relationship can be even better. Similarly, don't begrudge your partner for having past relationships that still mean a lot to them. Their attachment to their memories doesn't take away from your present.

Give your partner encouragement. When they try new things or are struggling at their job, boost them. Tell them that you are proud, and remind them that you believe in them. Everyone wants to know that they have people in their life who support them, and having their partner's support is often one of the most essential forms of support. Encourage them to do better at things they love and let them explore their passions.

Mary and Tim are a couple who have been married for forty years. One of the best things that they do for each is encouraging one another, and they attribute encouragement as the basis for their long love. Mary collects Halloween decorations, which she displays all year long, and Tim doesn't have the same passion. Still, he allows her to decorate certain spaces of their house with whatever decorations she wants, encouraging her passion, even if he finds it a little strange at times. Mary mutually allows Tim space for his sports memorabilia.

Prove that you are not taking your partner for granted by expressing acts of gratitude. It's not enough just to say that you are glad to have them in your life. You need to show it in a multitude of ways, and if you aren't saying it or showing it, your relationship will become strained, and you and your partner will grow apart. It only takes a little gratitude to prove your devotion and show your partner that you are willing to work to make your relationship function better than ever. Show your partner your appreciation every day. Find at least one thing about them to appreciate, and your relationship will be stronger than ever.

CHAPTER 4

Creating a Sense of Security in Your Relationship

The Differences Between Thoughts, Emotions, and Actions

Your thoughts, your emotions, and your actions all have various impacts on each other and your relationship. They each can fuel and be caused by insecurities, and as a result, they can make your relationship arduous. Too many people correlate these parts of themselves in ways that do more harm than good, but they each have unique qualities. They all influence one another, but having a bad thought doesn't mean that you will take harmful actions just as destructive thoughts don't always fuel harmful actions.

Thoughts are the dialogue that occurs in your head. Unconscious thoughts often fuel this dialogue. Emotions, meanwhile, are related to how you feel. You cannot control your feelings just as you cannot fully control your thoughts. Both go in and out of your head, and they can pass in and out without you realizing the more tremendous implications of them. Actions, meanwhile, are what you choose to do based on your thoughts and your emotions. If you have a harmful thought, you aren't necessarily going to resort to harmful action, and when you have harmful emotions, you may not think before acting on those feelings.

You must understand that your thoughts, actions, and emotions are entirely different entities. It would help if you differentiated your emotions, thoughts, and actions to ensure that you feel secure. If you have a thought that is something along the lines of, "My partner is going to leave me," you can take control of your actions and your feelings. You can remind yourself that you are not going to act on your insecurities. Further, you can sway your emotions through awareness. You can acknowledge that thoughts you are having are insecurities and not rational, which allows you to distinguish between how you think, how you feel, and how you act. The more you understand the relationship between what you feel, what you do, and what you think, the clearer your head will become. When you can consciously understand your relationship with your thoughts, emotions, and actions, they can no longer unconsciously control you.

How to Control Your Feelings

The short answer to how to control your feelings is that you cannot ever fully regulate them, but you can influence them. Feelings often make people feel powerless, but they should be an ally rather than an enemy. Sometimes, feelings will strike you, and there will be nothing you can do to get rid of them altogether, but that doesn't mean that you can't understand them and rationalize them. You can become conscious of your feelings and understand that they cannot influence your behaviors unless you let them do so. The more you practice managing your feelings rather than trying to run away from them, the easier it will be to reduce anxiety through the handling of your emotions.

Become more mindful of your feelings. Start learning how you feel and your feeling patterns. Become more aware of what you are really feeling. When you feel anger, evaluate if there is something more to your feeling than anger or if anger is the predominant feeling you have. Learn how you are feeling at this moment, and don't let yourself be influenced too much by the feelings of your past. Focus on what is happening mentally right now, and you will have more mindfulness.

Take time for meditation. Meditation is a great way to help you become more mindful. Meditation is the process of taking time from your busy day to balance your mind and find focus in the chaos. When you meditate, you dedicate time to yourself. You learn to let your thoughts exist without judgment, and you become altogether closer to yourself. People who meditate regularly see a myriad of health benefits, and tend to be less stressed than their non-meditating counterparts, so when you meditate, your anxiety levels will likely drop, even if you do none of the other steps in this book (though, you certainly should attempt the other steps as well for best results).

Find methods of creative expression. Finding a creative outlet for your feelings allow you to discover new ways to express your emotions that will enable you to create unique pieces. Writing or art are great options for people who need a creative outlet. You do not need to be "good" at these activities to have fun with them. Don't pressure yourself in these activities. Merely do the activities with only the will to express some of what you are feeling. Explore various creative outlets until you find one that feels right for you. There's no right or wrong hobby to choose. Just find an expressive method that speaks to you.

Take the pressure off yourself. If you're prone to pressuring yourself for everything from how you look to how you feel to how you act, you need to let up just a little bit. It is good to expect a lot of yourself and want to do your best, but when you put undue pressure on yourself, you send your emotions into chaos. They don't know how to respond, and they get confused. As a result, you get unclear signals, and you can't identify how you feel because you are feeling so much. Take a breath and let some of that pressure go away because the minute you do, your feelings won't be so messy. Your brain will start to find balance. You'll no longer feel stifled by your ambitions, and you'll be able to relax just a little.

Embrace the unexpected. Surprises are often bad ones, but they can also be exciting opportunities. With every unexpected event, even the bad ones, you are given new chances to make changes in your life. Marsha, who struggled in her relationship after her husband cheated, realized that she wanted to forgive her husband when Marsha's dad died. Upon her dad's passing, she realized that she didn't want to let her husband's mistake ruin twenty good years of marriage. Her dad's brother had been angry about a fight they had in their twenties. He'd come to the funeral, face full of regret, wishing he'd made amends while his brother was still alive. Marsha realized anger had consumed her. Not everyone would be as forgiving as Marsha, but she took her dad's death, and she used it as a reminder that life is too short to be bitter. She let her husband back into her life tentatively and she put in the work to fix the holes in their relationship.

Reduce the stressors in your life. Whether your relationship anxiety feeds your stress or your stress feeds your relationship anxiety, you need to get your stress levels under control. If certain activities or duties put your stress levels over the top, see if you can adjust them to be less stressful or get out of them altogether. If your boss has too high demands, which causes you to come home to your partner, feeling anxious and insecure, have a conversation with your boss, and see if you can establish a new work balance that will reduce your stress levels and make you feel more relaxed at home. When you can reduce stressors outside your relationship, you also reduce them within your relationship.

Practice deep breathing. For a few moments, focus on your breathing when you are feeling overwhelmed. When your feelings hang over you, and they are a chaotic storm, calm them through taking a deep breath and letting the oxygen surge through your body. Feel the energy of the air, and let it give you mental clarity and the strength you need to continue with your life, even as the emotions threaten to drown you. When you feel anxious, just take five minutes to breathe even more deeply. If it takes longer than five minutes to feel better, add another five minutes to your breathing. Keep adding more time until you are equipped to deal with your feelings.

Breathe through your feelings before you act. Return to those breathing techniques in the previous paragraph, and let them guide you as you turn your feelings into actions. When you are tempted to act on impulse, you'll want to pause before you act. Take time to separate your actions from your emotions. Remember that you do not need to do anything as an immediate response to your feelings. Take some time to contemplate whether you want to act to alleviate anxiety or if you want to act because you think your actions will improve your situation. If the answer is the former, resist action. If the answer is the latter, proceed to act, but do so with caution. Keep yourself in check as you act and be sure that your feelings aren't taking over.

Name what you are feeling. Find words to describe what you are feeling. You don't have to use basic terms, such as mad, sad, or joyous, but you can use those if they help. Find a way to pinpoint what it is that you are feeling, and put it into words as best as you can. Often, single-word terms will not suffice, but they can be a good starting point. You can start by saying that you feel sad, but then you can dig deeper and realize that you are devastated. From there, you can go even further and say, "My partner's actions profoundly hurt me because they have touched on some of my existing insecurities, and the insecurities I have make me feel shame and despair." Force yourself to identify what you are feeling.

Get to the heart of what you are truly feeling beneath your surface-level sensations. As in the exercise above, feelings are usually not just one word. They are typically complex and multi-faceted because of how they interact with one another and are fueled by our pasts. Find what is fueling that emotion the most and then try to pinpoint the other factors that have a role in that feeling. Understand how your emotions are so much more than they seem at first glance and don't let yourself only feel the top part of any emotion. Force yourself to go through every layer and to embrace what lies beneath.

Your feelings aren't something that you can control because they happen without you rationally choosing for them to commence. Nevertheless, you can shift your feelings through becoming more aware of your emotions and allowing your feelings to exist without judgment. Your feelings make or break your anxiety, so carefully nurture your brain so that your feelings lessen your anxiety instead of increasing it. Emotions are scary, especially if you have past trauma that worsens them, but they are never your enemy. They are part of you, which means they are something you can love.

Self-Awareness is Key

When you are self-aware, you take off your blinders and become more aligned with yourself. Self-awareness is the art of seeing who you are without the insecurities and self-delusions that usually cloud your vision. It is about being honest with yourself and loving yourself despite your flaws. Self-awareness is making unconscious parts of yourself conscious and understanding how those parts of you impact your relationship. There are so many reasons that you need to become more self-aware. The most important reason is that self-awareness starts a trend of self-acceptance and emotional stability. Self-awareness cannot hurt you. It can only make you a better version of yourself and show you the steps you need to take to master your situation. Self-awareness is one of the most essential tools you can use to stop letting your emotions dictate how you think and how you act.

The more you become self-aware, the less oblivious you will be to relationship woes. When you are self-aware, you can spot problems before they become worse. You are gifted with the skill of sensing the signs even when they are barely apparent. Your intuition will be fine-tuned, and you'll be able to feel that things are off before the problem becomes conscious, allowing you to address issues before they fester. Self-awareness is not just about yourself. It is about becoming more in tune with your surroundings and the people in your life as well. It is a skill that helps you look beyond yourself because you already understand yourself. You can then focus on everything else that influences your anxiety.

Self-awareness helps you make peace with yourself. When you are self-aware, you aren't automatically going to become self-assured, but you will be on a path towards self-confidence. Continued self-awareness helps you get to know yourself, and when you get to know yourself better, you have less to be insecure about. Thus, self-aware people do not become trapped in their personal emotional bubble, and they can more easily share how they feel and become communicative members of their relationships. When two people in a relationship are self-aware, it is like dynamite against relationship anxiety.

When you feel good about yourself, you're assured that you can handle whatever situation occurs.

When you're self-aware, you stop worrying so much about your deficiencies. What you can't do matters less because you know what you can do. You have taken stock of your strengths and weaknesses, and as a result, you know how to push forward and get the solutions you crave. Self-awareness promotes learning your shortcomings, but it doesn't emphasize them as things you need to hate about yourself. When you're self-aware, you should push towards self-love and acceptance because if you don't love yourself, you can't be fully aware. When you become self-aware, you create a new relationship with yourself, which helps you create a new dynamic with the rest of the world too, including your partner.

Ultimately, self-awareness allows you to clear some mental space for more important matters. You can focus less on your internal struggles, which gives you more time to tackle the insecurities you have about your relationship. Plus, when you are self-aware, you are thinking more with reasons, so you naturally do not worry as often. The more self-aware you are, the more liberated you will feel from the control your emotions have over you. You will take charge of your feelings and learn that there are better things to do than be anxious. Anxiety is a distraction from your real life, and there's so much more you can do when you say, "I do not want to be anxious anymore."

CHAPTER 5

Developing Self-Awareness

Become More Cognizant of Your Feelings

To preserve your relationship, you need to deal with your feelings, and you need to understand how they function. The more you understand your feelings, the better. One way to understand them is self-awareness, but there is so much more to discover about your feelings. Your feelings are the things that drive your behaviors and thought patterns. If you can get in charge of your emotions, you can take control of your anxiety and learn how to cope with it, even when it is at its most intense. If you're used to ignoring your feelings, it takes time to get back in touch with them and bring them to the surface, but anyone can understand their feelings and learn to handle them.

Journal every day. People who journal tend to be more self-reflective and feel more optimistic. Journaling is one of the best daily tasks that you can do to get in touch with your feelings. Keeping a journal allows you to keep track of how you are doing emotionally, and as you journal, you can start to see patterns that help you understand your relationship with yourself and your partner. People who journal are less anxious, less depressed, and they have better overall mental health. Accordingly, when you're self-aware, you're more equipped to maturely deal with relationship issues and know what your needs are in that relationship.

Discuss your emotions with your loved ones. Don't be afraid to be honest about how you feel. If you cannot be honest about how you feel, you are censoring major parts of yourself, which feels emotionally draining. If you feel angry about something, let that anger exist, and don't try to hide it from the people in your life. Having anger doesn't mean that you have to yell, but you should express those feelings somehow. For example, you can say, "I am upset about this because…" Through this method, you can temper your actions by staying in touch and open about your feelings. If you don't want to talk to your partner about how you feel right away, you can turn to someone like your best friend or a family member. As long as you aren't bottling your feelings up, you can control your emotions.

Stop demonizing your feelings. There's nothing wrong with whatever it is that you feel. People tend to treat their feelings as dirty or shameful. Your feelings are not in themselves evil. Even if you think evil things, those thoughts and their corresponding feelings aren't evil.

How you act on your emotions are what define you. There are no bad feelings; they are all part of the average human experience, so don't bully yourself over the feelings that you have. Embrace your feelings and allow them to be a neutral part of you that isn't bad or good. They just are, and trying to ignore their existence is only going to make you more anxious in the long run. Feelings are fleeting, but they are not unimportant.

Your feelings are important parts of you that you cannot alienate from yourself. When you try to shut down your feelings, all you accomplish is making yourself feel worse. Shutting down your feelings can even make you have increased anxiety and develop depression. Having a good relationship with your emotions is vital if you want to have a strong relationship with another human being. You'll want to encourage your partner to develop a better relationship with their feelings as well. Share these tips with them for the best results for you both.

Sit with Your Feelings

When you have negative feelings, you need to stop pushing them away and learn to exist with those emotions. Feelings do not go away just because you ignore them. Negative feelings only become more engrained when you ignore them, and positive ones become lost. Society often encourages people, especially men, to shut down their feelings and push them away in favor of rationality, but humans are nothing without our feelings. Emotions make us kind and empathetic even when it doesn't serve us to be that way. You need to learn to exist in the same body as your feelings because when you can sit with your feelings, you can conquer them and take control of yourself.

Know that you are more than your feelings. You are more than your sadness or contentment, and you are more than your rage or your joy. Your name is not anxiety. Your personality is not fear, and your eyes are not worry. You are so much more than the feelings you have, so do not let your emotions control how you feel about yourself. Don't call yourself a jerk because you feel angry or irrational sometimes. Don't think you are crazy because you let your insecurities make you feel anxious. Feelings are often a reflection more of your circumstances than you as a person. You inspire them, and they exist within you, but they definitely are not you. Let your identity be more than your worries.

When you feel a surge of emotions, give yourself five to ten minutes to process what you feel. Do not do anything major within those ten minutes. Impulses often go away when you give them time. You may feel anxious as you process your emotions, but this anxiety is necessary if you want to grow and become less anxious next time you have similar thoughts. Sitting with your feelings takes away the potency of those feelings, and it allows you to see them more clearly as the initial fervor of those feelings wears off. If within five to ten minutes, the emotions don't calm, take a breath and wait the feelings out a few more minutes and remind yourself that whatever is worrying you is not the end of the world.

Do not try to censor your emotions or try to make them less ugly. Feelings sometimes are ugly. They feel bad, and there's no way of making yourself think they are nice without self-delusion. If you have ugly feelings, exist with that ugliness. Remind yourself the ugliness is in your feelings alone and is not inherent in you. Be honest about what your feelings look like because if you're not, you're covertly ignoring them rather than sitting with them. You can't sit with someone you don't know. If you don't know someone, You're only sitting in the proximity of them. Before you can sit with your feelings, you have to introduce yourself and let them introduce themselves to you.

If you learn to sit with your feelings, they will have less control over you. Your anxiety will be that much easier to manage. Take the time to get to know your feelings because once you know them, they aren't so scary after all.

Be More Vulnerable

Vulnerability is the most valuable tool in any relationship, and it helps you become more self-aware of your own emotions and desires. When you are vulnerable, you deepen your connection with your partner, and your relationship feels stronger, which lessens your fears that it is fragile and might someday break.

When you are honest with others, they will be honest with you. When you take the risk of being honest with your partner, they will feel more willing to take that same risk with you, which will open up your communication and make you both happier and more secure in your relationship.

When you are honest with others, you are honest with yourself. As you know, it's important not to deceive yourself, and when you are vulnerable, it's hard to fool yourself because you are instead exposing parts of yourself that you would usually keep hidden.

When you are honest with others, you give your emotions the space they need. Your emotions have room to breathe when you release them from your body. They aren't caught in your body dor ruminating and fretting. They can leave you alone so that you can get more productive tasks done.

Vulnerability is all about honesty and allowing yourself to show your significant other parts of yourself that you hide from most of the world. It is about finding emotional intimacy and letting someone know you.

Talk About Your Feelings

You can't be self-aware if you refuse to admit your feelings, so start taking additional measures to facilitate conversations about your feelings with your partner. You know that communication is essential. Well, it's especially important when you have a whirlpool of emotions that make it hard for you to determine what is happening in your mind and how to respond to the anxiety that you feel. There's nothing that should be off the table when you talk to your partner about your feelings because you should feel secure enough that you can talk about anything with your partner. At least, you should feel that way once you have completed all the exercises in this book.

Do not be ashamed of what makes you happy. If something gives you joy and doesn't hurt anyone else, don't let anyone, especially your partner, make you feel silly about your interest. If you like a "trashy" reality TV show, own up to it and express your interest without shame. Shame prohibits genuine conversations, and it makes it hard for you to be honest with your partner. If they lightly joke about your interest, don't take the gesture too hard, but if the comment does bother you, explain that to your partner as well. Honesty reaps more honesty, so the more you practice sharing how you feel, the easier it will become.

Don't be afraid of broaching negative topics. Some tough conversations are hard to bring up. Nevertheless, when something is hard, that often makes it even more worthwhile to do. Talking about your feelings creates communication and opens up your relationship to so many possibilities. When you can talk about tough issues, you can solve them or at least address them. You can patch the holes in yourself and your relationship, which will obliterate your anxiety. If you can talk about your feelings, you show that you are willing to accept yourself, and to be self-aware, you need to accept yourself.

Acknowledge Your Mistakes and Flaws

You are not perfect, so quit the charade and learn to embrace your flaws. You don't have to be proud of your mistakes, but you do need to be able to admit that those flaws exist and that you have done wrong in the past. Your partner doesn't want a perfect partner. They want someone who will open up to them. They crave intimacy more than perfection because perfection doesn't exist, and it wouldn't be human if it did exist. Mistakes don't make you an immoral person. They're just part of being alive, and as long as you learn from your mistakes, you're living the right way.

Admit when you did something wrong or were unfair with your partner. When you fight with your partner, you're not always the one in the right. It may feel that way at the time, but you are often culpable for at least some of the escalation. Admit the parts that you were responsible for causing, and when you need to, apologize for inappropriate actions on your part.

Accept that you have downfalls just as your partner does. You both are an interesting duo, I'm sure. Your faults probably feed into each other, sometimes, but your strengths probably also make each other's faults better. At least, that's the case in a well-developed and communicative relationship. Let your partner help you with your downfalls rather than trying to hide those parts of yourself. A young woman I spoke to, Emily, had an alcohol addiction that she kept secret from her husband, Ryan, for a long time. Still, when she finally confessed her addiction to him, they were able to work together to pull funds so that she could begin a treatment program that changed their lives. Several months after her treatment, Emily then had to return the favor when Ryan's depression got worse. Their story shows that partners are stronger when they work together to handle issues.

Know that you are more than just your errors. Even if you've made terrible mistakes, you're not a lost cause. You're so much more than the bad things you've done. You can take the time to outweigh your mistakes with future positive actions. Don't keep making the same mistakes, and show yourself that you a better person now than ever before. In a relationship, it's rewarding to see your partner grow and become a better version of themselves, so allow your partner to be part of your development process.

People all make mistakes, and there's no reason to bully yourself over the fact that you are imperfect too. Your partner probably makes plenty of mistakes, and I'm sure you're aware, maybe too aware, of them, but you still love you're your partner despite those flaws. People are complicated, which makes it so rewarding to learn about them, and it makes life worth all the stress and hardship because the joy of companionship and love is more significant than anything else in life. You don't grow old without a few mishaps, so let yourself grow old.

Become More Mindful

Mindfulness is the practice of being present in the moment and becoming more aware of your surroundings. You've practiced mindfulness a little bit already, but if you are struggling to know how to be more mindful, you can use the following tips to establish a better mindfulness practice. When you are mindful, you will feel a nearly immediate difference in your anxiety levels.

Learn the signs that you're going to do something destructive. There's a certain feeling that consumes your body when you're going to do something that, at least on a subconscious level, you know is going to harm you or your relationship. Identify the signs of doing something you know you shouldn't, and resist your temptation when you feel the need to lash out and do something you know you'll regret.

Notice your feelings as they are growing. Feelings start as tiny inklings in the pit of your stomach, and they grow into much larger beings. If you're mindful, you can sense them as they start to emerge. You can feel as they begin to crescendo, but with your awareness, they won't inundate you as they grow. You can take a breath, and you won't feel that your feelings are choking you. Your mind will be clear, and you can coexist with your feelings.

Focus on what you feel now, not what you felt in the past or what you want to feel in the future. The present is what you can control, and it is what you need to define. The more mindful you become about your emotions, the easier they are to handle. Mindfulness is a simple concept that can be hard for people to execute when they've become detached from their present, either daydreaming too much about the future or being dragged backward by the past.

Self-Compassion Can Heal

Being more kind to yourself is one of the best methods you can use for self-awareness because when you are kind to yourself, the world becomes just a little brighter. When you're kinder to yourself, you're in the mental state to be more aware of yourself and give yourself some space and the encouragement you need to heal your anxiety. Do not underestimate the power being a little nicer to yourself can have on a relationship. Many of your insecurities and worries are probably rooted in self-esteem issues and your inability to treat yourself with self-compassion, which challenges your role in your relationship.

Treat yourself every once in a while. Let yourself have simple indulgences without feeling selfish or too needy. Everyone needs to indulge once in a while to show themselves the love that they deserve. Buy yourself that pair of shoes you had your eyes on or that watch. Let yourself have something nice, even if it isn't something that big. When you have an emotional need, give in to it, and let yourself have whatever it is that you need. If you neglect yourself, you will neglect your relationship as well. To have a strong relationship with someone else, you first need a strong relationship with yourself.

Tend to your needs first. Don't keep putting everyone else first. It can be tempting to always sacrifice for your partner, and I know you probably want to put them first. Still, if you are wearing yourself too thin, you're not going to be that helpful to your partner, and you're going to drag yourself down in the process, which will hurt your relationship. Make sure you are eating a balanced diet and getting time to relax and be by yourself. When you have a physical or emotional need, tend to that before tending to your partner when they can manage their own needs.

Forgive yourself. Whatever mistakes you have made in the past, especially ones in your relationship, you need to forgive yourself for those mistakes because holding onto the guilt is not helping you. Make amends and right your wrongs, but if your partner has forgiven you, there's no reason that you need to continue to beat yourself up over the past. Let yourself move on, and when you do that, you can do better going into the future and learn from your mistakes. Instead of making yourself feel guilty about what has already passed, do your best to do better and not make the same old mistakes.

It is beautiful to know how to be compassionate to yourself. Self-compassion is an underestimated virtue in society. People are often encouraged to put themselves last, and the value of self-sacrifice is furthered in stories. While sacrificing for others is a good virtue, it is hard to give anything to others if you are not giving yourself what you need. Be more considerate of yourself. Treat yourself as someone precious. On occasion, put yourself first to be in a better headspace that alleviates your anxiety and makes you feel self-assured.

CHAPTER 6

Beyond Therapy

While therapy may be a crucial practice for some couples, there are so many steps that you can take outside of therapy. These practices will help you reconnect with your partner without needing professional help. In the process, you will grow to feel more secure in your relationship and tackle issues that you and your partner need to address if you want to grow stronger. You do not have to tackle all these suggestions at once. Start slow and build up your relationship again at the pace that works for you. If you and your partner are both willing to give in to this process, you will see progress.

Rediscover What Makes You and Your Partner a Couple

Sometimes, partners can become disconnected from one another. When you sense distress in your relationship, you pull yourself away emotionally or physically to protect yourself from the potential emotional fallout that the issues in your relationship could cause. Sensing your distance, your partner can also become distant. As a result, you lose track of what makes you a couple, and you become a pair of individuals rather than a team, which is damaging to your relationship's future. Plus, distance makes anxiety more profound. Accordingly, it would be best if you found what makes you and your significant other a team. Revive what makes you a unit of individuals rather than individuals forced to be a unit.

Take a trip down memory lane. Look through your old pictures together or dig souvenirs from trips. Think about funny occasions at family dinners or remember the day when you first met. Take time to think about the past and remember what made your relationship so good back then. The more you can reflect upon the past, the better grip you can get on the future. Don't forget the foundation that you built back then because it is that foundation that will help you get through and continue to make beautiful memories together. If there wasn't something worth having in that relationship, you wouldn't have continued it, so remember why it all began.

Remember the good times fondly and honor the bad times. Look at the past fondly, but don't wash away all the struggles you had. Struggles are essential fibers in the fabric of relationships. They can make your relationship healthier, and they show you that your relationship is worth fighting for. While it's nice to think of the good times that made your relationship so great, you also need to honor the bad experiences you had together. These experiences didn't necessarily make your relationship stronger, but they are critical because you got through them, even if only by the skin of your teeth. The moments of survival show that you can make it through hardships. You have the will and the might to do what you need to do to push through your difficulties. There have been times when you probably nearly fell apart, but you kept yourself and your relationship together, and you can do it again. All you have to do is find that energy and spirit again.

Continue practices that you did when you first started dating. Go on little dates to the café down the street.

Have a date night! No matter how long you have been in a relationship, you cannot drop the little gestures that were so important when you first started dating. You should continue to date. Of course, the way you date will have changed, but you need to make time for just you and your partner: no kids, no friends, and no work calls. Detach from everything else and reconnect with your partner. Even just a once a week or once a month outing can refresh your relationship and reduce worries.

Some things stay the same, some things change, but that's okay. You'll have new things that unify you, such as children, dreams of the future, or homeownership. These things mark new ways that you are a team, and they do not outweigh the old parts of yourselves that were a team, but they are essential to consider and respect. Think of all the things you and your partner bond over and find ways to make those things a more significant part of your relationship. Don't focus on just one area, such as money, but find connections in all aspects of your lives.

Reviving that old spirit in your relationship is a great way to remember why you're together in the first place. When you forget about your past and all the things that make you a team, you lose so many of the facets of a relationship that help both partners feel secure in that relationship. As a result, when you don't pay homage to the history of your relationship, your efforts at improving your relationship are too quickly derailed by insecurity.

It doesn't take a lot of effort to rediscover what makes you a couple, but it takes effort that many people refuse to invest because of busy lives. You aren't too busy to save your relationship.

Be More Positive

Research from John Hopkins suggests that people who have a more positive attitude are less likely to have heart conditions, and they are more likely to live longer. They are also more likely to have less anxiety, depression, and insomnia. The research on positivity overwhelmingly shows that when you are positive, you feel better, which means you have better odds of having the mental and physical health that you need to deal more adequately with relationship anxiety. While it is just a small step in improving your relationship, if you can believe that you can do better and that you can feel better about your romance, you will in time.

Realize that cynicism is an unhealthy coping mechanism. When you are cynical, you expect the worst because you figure that it will hurt less if you are disappointed if you don't have hope. Still, unfortunately, cynicism leads to self-sabotage and unhappiness. When you are cynical, you are more likely to experience the things you are afraid of because you don't believe that you can do anything better. When you don't believe in something, you unconsciously turn yourself off from that notion, which means you can never accomplish anything more. Being jaded isn't a sign of maturity. It just means that you aren't coping correctly, and it prohibits you from advancing.

Stop expecting the worst. Whatever it is that loops in your mind as the worst-case scenario may not even happen, and often, your worst-case scenario is overblown and makes situations feel more hopeless than they are. Your situation is not so dire that you cannot have hope. Even if your relationship is on the edge of complete destruction, with the will to improve it, you can find solutions. There's no relationship, other than a toxic or abusive one, that isn't salvageable. While bad things can happen, expecting them to happen doesn't get you anywhere. If your relationship ends, you'll still hurt. Guarding your expectations won't make the heartache go away when things go wrong, so give yourself some slack and let yourself have hope.

It's okay to be hopeful. Hope doesn't make you naïve. A person without hope is an empty shell of themselves, and they can never reach what they want to achieve. Hopeless people see no need to make goals. They don't have ambition. They are depressed and in despair. They feel empty with no way of being fulfilled. Do you want that to be you? Of course, not. Hope is not a dangerous thing to have; instead, not having hope is the actual danger. Humans are meant to hope. They are built to believe, dream, and create a future that is different from the present, and that is hope. Hope is believing but not knowing that your relationship can make it.

Go to sleep, thinking about all the good things that can happen with a new day. When you go to sleep on a good note, you become more positive. Don't let your last thoughts be ruminations about everything that went wrong with your partner that day. While it is crucial to acknowledge the negative parts of your relationship, before you go to sleep is an unideal time for such contemplation. Research shows that the thoughts you have before you go to sleep highly influence what you do when you are awake because just before you go to sleep, you enter a hypnotic-like state, which makes your unconscious brain more susceptible to suggestion. Thus, just before you sleep, your unconscious mind is like a sponge and better absorbs the information you give it.

Find the silver lining in even the worst of situations. Get in the habit of seeing the good aspects of difficult situations rather than deciding the situation is not worth dealing with anymore because of how dire it has become. The positives don't have to outweigh the negatives, but you do need to focus on those positives. When you focus on positives, you focus on what you can control rather than what you can't, and you start to fix your bad situation rather than harping on all the chaos of it. For seasoned cynics, it can be hard to rewire your brain to think more positively but start by forcing yourself to find little bright parts in otherwise darkness.

Start seeing the tiny good things that build up to make substantial, good things. To find the silver lining, it helps to see how little bits of goodness can create incredible things. Humans aren't born fully formed. We begin as little, and as we grow older, we are fed by little bits of our environments, which shape who we become. No person is created without context, and all things in life are build of small pieces. If you cracked open your phone, you'd find that it contained a plethora of tiny parts that individually aren't that remarkable. Little things and little gestures become much more prominent when you start to see how quickly they add up. One dollar doesn't seem like much, but one dollar a day for a year is $365.

You hurt yourself when you refuse to be positive, and you hurt your partner. Your negativity is contagious. When you are negative, your partner will become more cynical, and your partner's negativity will make your negativity worse! Negativity always leads to unhappiness because you cannot see the good inherent in the world. You don't see how all those little things add up to be remarkable things. You miss all the aspects that could save your relationship and pay way too much attention to parts that could, but won't definitely, destroy it. Negativity is a blinder that makes it hard to see the world clearly, and you don't need more blinders than you already have.

Don't just be more positive in your relationship. Be more positive about everything. Your whole outlook on life should be brighter. When you feel good about things outside your relationship, you also feel good about things within your relationship.

Positivity spreads, so let it spread. When you are positive, you share good energies with the world, and these energies allow you to connect with your partner and feel happier. When you are positive, and your partner is positive, your anxiety is immediately reduced. You can then start to take action with a clear mindset that is not clouded by your cynicism. Cynicism cannot save a relationship, but positivity can lead the way to make profound changes that ensure both you and your partner are content. If you tend to be negative, positivity can be challenging, but it is something that you need to create.

Address Fears of Abandonment

One of the most significant relationship anxiety triggers is the fear of abandonment. One of the most driving fears in relationship anxiety is the fear of abandonment. People who have been abandoned, physically or emotionally, in the past may have a persistent insecurity that their partner will not love them forever. Love is complicated, making it a huge risk to start a relationship, but the rewards are so much greater. If you ever want to escape your romantic anxiety, you must learn to address any fears of abandonment that you have. Resiting them is the best way to fight your worries because most relationship fears come down to not wanting to be rejected or hurt.

Think about your past. When did you feel abandoned in your past? Were you a kid whose parent left? Did you have a significant death of a character? Did a partner of a past relationship leave you in a bad situation? Many people have multiple instances of abandonment that make them more worried about being rejected by their partner. Abandonment doesn't mean that someone just walks away. It can mean much more than having your parent walk out and never come back when you were a kid. Death can feel like abandonment to a child, and that feeling can go into adulthood. Additionally, having a parent who worked long hours and was hardly ever home can feel like abandonment. Any instance that made a person feel like they weren't being cared for or tended to can translate as abandonment. Even if you don't feel like you have been abandoned, upon reflection, you can discover that you may still have some abandonment issues.

Choose to take an emotional risk of love. Make love a choice. Don't let yourself be powerless in your relationship. If you make the conscious choice to risk your heart, you are putting your fears into your control. You're telling your anxiety that it cannot stop you from being happy and in love. Most of all, you allow yourself to be vulnerable, which is a crucial act in any secure relationship. Love may end in heartache, but along the way, you will experience irreplaceable joys. As the adage goes, "It's better to love and lost than never to have loved at all." Love is hard to manage, but wouldn't life be awful without it?

Remember the constants of your life. These constants remind you that there are things that can endure. Everyone needs parts of their lives that they know will remain true. Maybe you know your mom will always love you or your best friend. Maybe you know you can always pet your dog, and he'll cuddle you gladly. Maybe you know that you can always trust yourself to survive. Your values and your beliefs are often parts of yourself that are constant. Trust in these constants and let them make you feel secure enough to dive into situations that are not as certain. Nothing worth having doesn't require at least a little risk, so stop playing it safe, and open up your heart.

Acknowledge that sometimes people leave. While many people will stay, there will always be some who leave, and you can't let that influence your self-worth. When people leave you, it does not mean that you are somehow deficient. People leave for several reasons, and it doesn't mean you're not worth enduring love or the effort. You are worth it, and if someone leaves, it's because you and that person are no longer compatible, or you are better apart. Sometimes, relationships fizzle out, and it is no one's fault. It's just something that happens, and it's not something that you should try to control or that should turn you off to the idea of love altogether.

When you feel abandoned or rejected, question those feelings. Is it a valid fear, or does it stem from insecurities about yourself? Most of the time, your worries are rooted in the things you don't like about yourself. Perhaps, you think your body is too fat, or you think you're stupid. These insecurities can make you think, "No one would want to stick around to be with someone like me." Unfortunately, the one who doesn't want to stick around is you. You don't want to be with yourself because, for whatever reason, you have internalized negative messages that cripple your self-esteem. Self-hate is common among people who cannot open up and fear that their partner will reject them and realize that they are not worth sticking around for. You cannot leave yourself, but when you wish you could, you expect that no one will stay.

Don't leave someone just because they might leave you. That's counterintuitive! Don't end a relationship first because you're so scared that someone is going to hurt you. You might get hurt, but you'll definitely be hurt if you don't give your relationship a chance to thrive and naturally run its course. Think about relationships that you feel could have been more but ended because of your fears. Those relationships weren't given a chance to be secure. You quit them before you could explore what they meant to you, and that's always more heartbreaking than a relationship that naturally runs its course.

If you have a history of abandonment or a fear of it, you need to address that fear. The same is true of your partner if they have these issues. If you both worry about being abandoned, you'll have a good understanding of what one another is feeling. In any case, fears of abandonment make it hard to be open and to discuss your worries. You'll be more prone to self-censorship, and there will always be a distance in your relationship until you can open yourself up just a little bit more. You are worth being vulnerable. You are worth the risk of love. Even if you don't feel worthy, you deserve the relationship you've always dreamed about and to feel secure in that relationship.

Express Understanding

Show that you understand your partner or that you are willing to try to understand. I have discussed this topic briefly in previous chapters. Still, if you want to avoid therapy or if you need additional help beyond therapy, you need to put an even greater effort into understanding them. Take the following steps to be sure your partner feels tended to and knows that you are willing to let their emotions become part of yours. In a relationship, you can never isolate your feelings from the other person's emotions.

Allow your partner time to talk, and as they talk, do not think about your side. Just listen. When you're listening, you don't need to think about how you're going to dispute them or about how you feel. Let your thoughts come organically, and delay your response until they have said what they needed to say. Authentic listening requires mindfulness, and you need to be present in the conversation without letting all your other thoughts drag you out of the moment. You'll never understand anyone unless you take the time to absorb what they are saying without your own perspective standing in the way. You'll always have a bias, but you can lessen it through consciousness.

As you listen, learn to reflect what your partner is saying. Don't just follow up what they're saying with "Okay, but I think…" Use words like, "It seems to me that you've been feeling this way…" and show that you are trying to understand. Give your partner time to correct what you think they are feeling and clarify where clarification is needed. Let their words shape your mindset rather than your prejudgments. You may know your partner well, but listening to their words is the best way to get to know them. As they speak, you may notice that they are deceiving themselves at times. You can address those issues later, but at first, try to understand what they are saying with clarifying questions and reflection before you break it all down.

Don't assume what they are feeling without hearing them out. It would help if you took the time to learn that information, not assume it. Never be dismissive of your partner's feelings. It doesn't matter if your partner is not rational; you can never be dismissive. Listen and let them get what they are feeling off their chests. By doing that, you can feel closer to them, and they will be more likely to be honest with you when they know that you can listen without too many judgments.

Be empathetic with your partner, but you need to try to feel their pain and other emotions to understand them. It's okay not always to get it, but do your best to walk in their shoes and to learn what it must be like for them. They may have challenges that you never realized before you did some additional investigating and tried to be empathetic.

You need to prove that you are willing to understand your partner. If you cannot sh0w that you are ready to do that, you will never get anywhere. Show that you can understand more than your own feelings. Your partner's feelings should matter to you. If you don't, that shows that your relationship is seriously disconnected and that your anxiety is rooted in a real sense of relationship danger. Put yourself out on a limb, and as you're on that limb, force yourself to share, but also force yourself to listen because you need both to do well in any relationship.

Use Natural Remedies

Becoming more in tune with nature can be cathartic for both you and your partner. The curative elements of nature are often neglected, and many people don't realize the fantastic properties of being outdoors. One couple, Julie and Sharona, found themselves paying more attention to their phones than each other. Both of them worked in marketing, and they felt like they were always on call. Julie started scuba diving, and she found that the activity eased her tension, so she shared the activity with Sharon. They now use scuba diving as a way to reconnect with each other and disconnect from the chaos of their busy lives.

Go on nature walks or hikes together, or do whatever else connects you to nature. Let the fresh air soothes your worries. Being outdoors can feel free, and it can take some of the tension from your mind. When you are outside with someone you love, you can leave behind the material worries of the world and focus on each other. Maybe you don't consider yourself an outdoorsy person, but just stepping out onto a balcony and breathing in the fresh air is a start. You don't have to go camping or mountain climbing to get in touch with nature. Anyone can add more of the natural world to their daily lives to be liberated from the bonds of material objects, work, and other non-natural pressures.

Use soothing herbs such as lavender or chamomile. These herbs are known for reducing anxiety, and using them in teas or through essential oils may make you feel calmer all around, which will lessen the stress you have about your relationship. There are dozens of other herbs that you can try for different ailments, both mental and physical, and herbs can help you feel more aligned with yourself and your partner.

Put away your phones and enjoy each other's company. Stop checking your email every five minutes and invest quality time with your partner. If you're always looking at your phone when you spend time with your partner, you are not giving quality time. You are distracted and potentially dismissive of your partner's emotional needs when your eyes are glued to your phone. You don't always need to put your phone away around your partner, but take some time to be phone free and enjoy each other's company because by doing that, you will build your relationship.

It may seem basic to go outside and enjoy nature, but research has found that people who are outdoors often are less anxious, and they have improved mood! The natural world has so many curative wonders that can help take some of the pressure off your relationship. Don't force yourself to try any natural activities that you don't enjoy, but do at least something to find connection with the world outside your technological bubble. Disconnection from the unnatural world allows you to connect to your partner, and it gives you time to work on your relationship woes.

Rebuild Fragmented Parts of Your Relationships

Over time, parts of every relationship get fragmented, which causes issues that lead to anxiety. You'll start to disagree about things that you never disagreed about before. You won't see eye to eye on matters that once bonded you. You'll drift apart as fragments get in the way of your continued relationship health. All the things you stopped understanding about each other must be understood once again. As you do this, you will learn to bridge your disconnections and differences of opinions. Ultimately, you must rebuild misunderstandings into understandings, and when you do, you will feel less anxious.

Start making connections that bridge your past selves with your present selves. You aren't who you were with the past, but you aren't a totally new person either, and your partner should recognize that. Discover the ways you are both the same and different, and allow those forms of yourself to coexist. Be open to changing dynamics because that's the only way forward.

Leave behind any bitterness. If you're bitter about something, there's no chance that you will move forward. Major hurts in your relationship are hard to get over, but if you want to maintain the relationship, you need to get over them, or they will always loom over you and your partner. You and your partner can't keep hanging old issues over one another's head. Letting go will not only help your relationship, but it will support your personal wellbeing. Holding onto hurts isn't making the other person pay. Most of all, it is making you suffer more than anyone else.

Say sorry for your wrongdoings. Your pride may struggle to utter the words, "I am sorry," but in a healthy relationship, those words are necessary. Don't say sorry just for the sake of it, but when you sincerely feel guilty for doing something wrong in your relationship, sorry is one of the simplest ways to express your regret and your desire to get better.

Stop trying to control the other person. You can't force them to participate more. You can ask them to do so, but you cannot force anything to happen that they don't want to happen, so you need to be patient and allow your partner to make their own choices, or they will feel stifled. Don't force a connection where it doesn't belong. It is the best feeling to connect to someone, but you can't make it happen no matter how hard you try.

Maintain healthy boundaries and repair broken boundaries. In any relationship, boundaries are essential. Both you and your partner need to have limitations that you keep up to feel safe in the relationship. Boundaries make sure that you don't become overly reliant on one another and that you have a sense of self beyond your partner. If you don't know who you are outside your relationship, of course, you're going to have increased anxiety because you cannot fathom who you would be beyond that relationship.

You need to make efforts to rebuild your relationship because when you have anxiety, you undoubtedly have relationship damage you need to address. Start learning how to deal with the past and bring into your present. You need to rectify what was with what is if you want any hope of feeling better about your relationship.

CHAPTER 7

Communication is Key to a Happy Relationship

They say, "Location, location, location," about finding suitable properties in the real estate world. Still, in the relationship world, we say, "Communication, communication, communication," because of how important it is if you want to maintain healthy and secure relationships. When you have strong communication, your relationship is more resilient to anxiety because you can express concerns in a health and mature manner.

Self-Disclosure

Self-disclosure means that you reveal information about yourself to your partner without them having to dig to get more information. You are upfront with parts of your life that you may be tempted to keep to yourself. For example, if one partner cheats on the other partner, self-disclosure would be admitting to the affair before the other partner found out about it themselves. While self-disclosure doesn't make up for the breach of trust, it is a good tool in a relationship because it allows you to bring something up first and admit to your issues before your partner discovers them on their own in less than ideal circumstances. Disclosure isn't just for unfortunate occurrences like infidelity, though. It can be used in several ways to promote relationship security.

You can self-disclose past actions. You may want to disclose some things that happened even before you were with your current partner. For example, you may want to talk about the horrific relationship you had with your dad, or you may want to confess that you were not faithful to a partner in the past, even though you have been faithful in the past. Other parts of yourself you may want to disclose are your sexuality. Maria spent years hiding from her husband that she was bisexual, which made her feel like she had to hide huge parts of herself. When she finally disclosed to Aaron that she had also dated women in the past, she felt relief filling her, and Aaron also felt better because the secrecy was gone.

You can also disclose your dreams and ambitions. If your partner doesn't know your hopes for the future, it may be hard to establish a future that makes both of you happy. You should feel comfortable discussing your ambitions with your partner, even if they are unlikely to come true. It is disingenuous to hide parts of yourself that make you most passionate, and a disconnect will inevitably arise. When partners can share their hopes for the future, they can envision how those hopes can interact with one another and be part of their overall relationship. Your dreams won't always come true, but it's still nice to share them with someone who will want them for you as much as you want them for yourself.

Disclose your dislikes as well as what interests you. If you don't like a meal that your partner makes, express that you don't care for that particular meal and tell them why. Often, it helps to ensure them that it isn't a matter of their skills as a cook. Rather, it is a matter of your tastebuds. Allow them to continue making those foods, but find a compromise so that you can have something you like on the table as well. Additionally, this same issue often comes into play with home décor. Couples have different styles, and while you have to give in in some décor areas and make compromises, neither of you should have a home full of pieces that you hate, which is why disclosing when you don't like something is so vital.

Most importantly, disclose your feelings and emotions. Your feelings and emotions are both parts of you that you probably keep to yourself far too much. Your partner can't know how you feel unless you tell them. When you're having a bad day, don't act like you're okay just because you don't want to drag down the mood. Allow yourself to relish in your partner's good mood while still allowing yourself to express that your day hasn't been so upbeat. At the very least, let your partner know how you are feeling. You don't have to elaborate more than that, but admitting to your feelings is an important step forward.

The more you can disclose, the closer your relationship will become because self-disclosure is an integral part of communication. The more you practice self-disclosure, the less odd it will feel, and as you do it more, your relationship will benefit. Conversations that felt impossible before will be a breeze, and your partner will get to know you better when you let them into your life. You give them parts of you that are precious, and you provide them with the opportunity to treat those delicate parts with careful hands. Self-disclosure is a gift, and it is a proactive action that can help you get ahead of your anxiety.

Rewards of Self-Disclosure

You let yourself be vulnerable rather than closed off. You open your heart, and you risk being rejected as we all do when we are vulnerable. Vulnerability is so essential, and when you self-disclose your feelings, past, and everything else that you need to talk about, you become more vulnerable. You let your partner into your innermost world, which translates into saying, "I trust you with parts of myself that could destroy me if used against me." You stop closing yourself off and running away from what makes you feel anxious, and you face the truth without letting yourself turn away from yourself and your relationship.

Your partner is more likely to be vulnerable to you. When you are vulnerable, you form intimacy with your partner. When you feed that intimacy into your relationship, you are likely to get out what you give in. Feeling closer to you, your partner will feel more comfortable disclosing parts of themselves and being honest about things they have been keeping from you, whether consciously or unconsciously. You both feel closer to one another as a result, which encourages you both to continue to be open to one another. It can be hard to take the step to openness, but someone has to start the journey first, and it might as well be you because nothing will change unless you put yourself on a limb.

Secrets never fester. If you practice self-disclosure, secrets aren't going to drive a wedge into your relationship. Secrets are some of the worst things that couples can keep from each other because they create separation rather than connection, and the person who is carrying the secret often feels ashamed of what they are keeping to themselves, which destroys their mental health and ability to engage in a relationship even further. Secrets can be tempting, but they don't do much good in the long run, and they don't create a trusting relationship, which leads to insecurity and anxiety.

You don't become bitter. If you have no secrets and have no disconnect, it's hard for bitterness to last. When you haven't faced the stale air between you and your partner, you are bound to feel chronic bitterness, which never allows your relationship to heal from past mistakes. Resentment is not a productive feeling. In a vengeful way, it can feel rewarding, but it creates no progress. It does not allow you to move on, which means that it will always hurt you. Bitterness isn't going to make your partner pay for their misdeeds. You're the one who pays, so move on and decide what moving on means for your relationship.

Your relationship continues to be on equal footing. Self-disclosure is a great way to ensure that your relationship has comparable power dynamics and reiterate that no one person is more invested than the other. When you take the time to self-disclose, you choose to restate your trust in your partner. You let them into your world, and they let you into theirs.

You Can Build Listening Skills

Start small and take at least fifteen minutes to have an uninterrupted conversation with your partner per day. If you already do this, great; add another fifteen minutes. If you don't do this, it's an easy way to become more connected to your partner in a matter of days. When you have these conversations, don't have your phone out. Sit down, turn the TV or other media off, and listen. There are so many parts of life that normally distract people from have dedicated conversations, so get rid of as many of those distractions as possible and commit to those fifteen minutes.

Don't try to dominate the conversation. When you're communicating, you don't want to make the conversation all about yourself. Amy and Allen were a couple who had this exact problem. Allen would come home from work, and as Amy tried to tell him about everything that went wrong with her day, Allen would unconsciously dismiss her by trying to "top her issues with ones he thought were more important." It took Allen a while to accept that he tended to talk more than listen, but as he began to self-reflect, he realized that listening to his wife more was good for both of them. No partner can dominate the conversation at all times. You both need to talk about yourselves, as individuals and as a couple.

Know that some days your partner will need to talk more, and you'll need to talk less. Good conversations don't mean that you each have to say the same amount. You should have balance, but every conversation doesn't require equal times in both the speaking and listening roles. If you're having the worst day of your life, your partner may put their issues on the back burner for a while, and you should do the same when your partner is having a dreadful day. You don't have to lie about how you are feeling, but you can benefit from keeping the focus on your partner when they need it. Relationships are all about give and take. Ensure that you are giving as much as you take.

Encourage your partner to listen to you because they need to hear you out as well. Express your need to be heard and understood. Expect them to give you dedicated time without distraction just as you plan on giving them. To help this process along, you can share this book with them or even just relevant parts of this book to understand what it takes to have solid communication skills and listen to one another. Explain to them how vital listening is for your relationship because if you don't start listening more, you will have no chance of reducing your relationship anxiety.

Sometimes venting is necessary, and it usually is just letting thoughts and emotions out, so don't make judgments or comments when you think your partner is being unfair. Hear them out, and let them get their feelings off their chests. There will be days when you need to get something off your chest, and those days are a great chance to practice listening. Vent sessions don't have to be rational, but they still are pretty cathartic. Sometimes communication isn't just having deep, heart to hearts. Sometimes, the best relationship communication is the moments when you let them complain about their boss for half an hour without trying to run away. You listen even though there are things you'd rather do. That's the most rewarding type of conversation a person can have— when you can just listen and take the words in without needing all the meaning in the world. Often, communication is more about emotions than taking a rational approach.

Practice communication skills with people who aren't your partner. While you want to focus on how you communicate with your partner, you may have similar communication patterns with other people. You can learn from how you talk to other close loved ones what you need to improve on with your communication. You can start to see what you tend to hold back and when you tend to get defensive. The more you understand how you communicate and practice using better skills, the easier it is for you to apply those techniques to your relationship and communicate in healthy ways.

The more you learn to listen, the more secure your relationship will become. Let your listening skills grow because when you do, your life will change, and you will engage with the world in ways that you only dreamed you could. Most importantly, you will have less to worry about in regards to your relationship. You'll be able to speak and listen without worrying that your relationship is falling apart. You'll feel closer to your partner than ever before. But listening is a lot harder than just choosing to hear. It requires knowing the difference between genuine listening and pseudo listening.

Pseudo Listening vs. Real Listening

Pseudo listening is self-serving listening that doesn't require much effort. It is the kind of listening you do when you are only half paying attention. You don't commit fully to the listening process, and you focus more on what you want to get out of the conversation than what you want to give in. You become selfish when you pseudo listening because listening is merely something you have to endure before you can say your piece. You are not deciding that you genuinely want to understand your partner's perspective. You are stuck in your mindset, and you don't care to be open to what anyone else might think.

When you pseudo listen, you may be thinking about what you might say next. You'll spend the whole time the other person is talking, thinking about how you are going to make your argument. You lose track of what the other person is saying because you're in your head, analyzing how to win the verbal back and forth you and your partner are having. Conversations are not competitions. They are not meant to be won and lost, which means that you are hurting your communication by trying to plan your thoughts. You're making it next to impossible to get anywhere because you refuse to look beyond your own mind.

You may have prejudgments that rule your thoughts about what your partner is saying. When you go into a conversation thinking you already know what you are going to get out of it, you are ruining the constructive influences of that conversation. You are assuming that you already know what the other person means without hearing out what they really mean. You are dismissing them before they have even said anything! One couple, Mark and Connor, did this to each other all the time. Mark would talk about how he was concerned about ho much Connor was going out with his buddies, and Connor always assumed that Mark was just being jealous. In actuality, Mark was hurt more than jealous and was feeling lonely; meanwhile, Connor spent so much time with his friends because he felt like he had nothing separate from Mark. Neither man could communicate their perspective because they went into conversations thinking they already knew everything there was to know. Their relationship, unfortunately, ended in divorce because they were never able to reconcile their separate perspective and were driven apart by their fears.

Pseudo listeners may be thinking about other things or trying to multitask. You'll all probably conversed with someone who seemed like they would rather be anywhere else when they were talking to you. You can't expect to listen if you are on your phone, typing up a work email or reading a news article. People are notoriously bad at multitasking. The fact of the matter is that the human brain is wired to focus on one thing at a time. You do better work when you can do just one task at that moment because you don't have to split your brain and try to handle several tasks at once. The same is true with conversations. You cannot be focused on what another person is saying if you're also trying to focus on something else. Give your full concentration to your partner for a few minutes each day to make sure that you have genuine listening at least daily. Not all conversations can have genuine listening but dedicate genuine listening to as many as you can

When you pseudo listen, you miss out on some of your partner's primary concerns. Your partner is trying to tell you something when you speak to them, and when you already think you know where the conversation is headed, you're not going to listen carefully. You'll take their words to mean one thing when, upon genuine listening, you'll realize that your partner meant something entirely different. Pseudo listening is never going to give you the full story. It will always create a false perspective of what is going on between you and your partner. When you pseudo listen, you rely on narratives from events and talks that have happened in the past, and these narratives don't always fit what is presently happening or what your partner is trying to express.

Genuine listening allows you not to be solipsistic. It's normal for you to struggle to see the world from other people's perspectives, but when you become solipsistic, you can only see the world through your perspective and struggle to fathom how other people, your partner included, don't see the world in that same way. You look at the world using a pair of wonky glasses that magnify certain things but deemphasize others. You do not see what it is. You see what you expect, and real conversations require you to challenge your expectations and date to see beyond your glasses.

When you listen genuinely, you let yourself be mindful about your conversation. You live in the moment, and you take in the stimuli around you as it happens. Your mind isn't on the fight you had yesterday or what this conversation will bring tomorrow. You're thinking about your feelings and reactions right now. You're trying to take in what your partner is saying without casting unfair judgments. You are present, and that's one of the best ways to start actively listening.

Genuine listeners don't feel the need to talk over their partners. You don't have to be the biggest voice in the room. Don't keep feeling the need to be the loudest one in any conversation because your voice volume doesn't reaffirm what you are saying, and it doesn't make you more conversational. If you're trying to talk over your partner, you are missing the point of listening. You are actively choosing not to listen at all by trying to drown out your partner's thoughts. Such actions are bound to cause trouble and make it harder for you to get anywhere with your relationship.

If you listen genuinely, you're open to conversations and their surprises. You may think that you listen to your partner, but there's likely a lack of listening somewhere if you have anxiety issues. You may utilize real listening in some circumstances but use pseudo listening in others. Become more aware of your listening patterns and find ways to genuinely listen more often.

Pseudo Listening Blocks Real Listening

When you pseudo listen, your partner can sense your lack of attention. When you aren't listening, people know it. Even if they aren't consciously aware that you are distracted, they can sense it unconsciously, which leads to several unconscious messages being formed. You can't ever fully get away with pseudo listening. It may be appropriate at a party when you're talking to someone you've met twice and trying to be friendly, but with someone you're supposed to know incredibly well, pseudo listening feels dismissive and hurtful. Additionally, it makes your relationship feel like it is in danger, creating the insecurity that leads to relationship anxiety.

Your partner will not want to be as open with you if you pseudo listen. No one wants to be vulnerable to someone who doesn't seem to care, and when you pseudo listen, the other person will think that you don't care about what they are saying. If you're spilling your heart out, and someone is yawning in the corner, you're going to feel like a fool, and when being vulnerable, that's the worst feeling in the world. Think of times you felt people haven't responded well to your vulnerability, and remember how awful that feels. That feeling is the one you create when you don't rise above pseudo listening! Don't waste your partner's vulnerability by not caring, and remember that what may not feel vulnerable to you may be vulnerable to your partner.

Pseudo listening makes it impossible to have empathy. You cannot feel what someone else is feeling if you don't let those feelings become a part of you. Absorb your partner's feelings, and let them guide your conversation. Use the emotional energies to help you establish a better understanding of your partner's worldview. Not only does listening help you save your relationship, but it makes you a more empathetic person in everything you do, and the world could use a lot more empathy.

The more you pseudo listen, the more you will feel a disconnect in your relationship. You and your partner will go through the motions with regular listening, but you will never do more than scratch the surface. You will be stuck having conversations that mean very little to either of you, which is discouraging in romantic relationships. When you cannot find anything more in your relationship, you feel stuck, and you want to escape the same old same old that has you stuck. Break through the monotony by allowing genuine conversations that feed you and your partner's souls. While it sounds challenging to reconnect with your relationship, it's not as bad as you think.

Don't think that hearing is enough. It doesn't matter if you can recite what another person said exactly, if you're not opening your mind to those words, you are not listening. Listening is not about hearing the words themselves or absorbing them. It is being able to know what those words mean to the other person. It is the joy of taking the time to treat a person's words (or nonverbal expressions) with care. There are some things that you will never fully understand about your partner, but you can do your best to try. Trying communicates a lot to your partner. It shows that you care enough to put in an effort, and it shows that you are willing to see things their way, even if you can't ever agree with that perspective.

Pseudo listening is not empathetic. You do not feel what it is like to walk in another person's shoes. You are listening to your feelings and nothing beyond that. You may sympathize with your partner, but you cannot understand how they feel until you take the time to learn through listening. Pseudo listening does not mean you are heartless and don't care for your partner. It only means that you are not trying to understand what it is to be them. For example, your partner comes home is upset over a minor ticket they got from a police officer. They may be incredibly upset, and if you aren't listening to why they are upset and how upset they are, you may never understand those feelings and shrug their experience off, saying, "It's no big deal," even though that's not what they wanted or needed to hear.

People who pseudo listen can't have fulfilling conversations. While you can still have conversations with meaning, you will never get full fulfillment from your conversations unless you take the time to listen genuinely. When you pseudo listen, you do not hear the things that go unsaid. You are not letting yourself sense the emotional charge behind the words or the cracks in your partner's voice; instead, you are warping your listening with your assumptions and what you believe your partner must be saying. It's easier that way, but it doesn't feel good. There's some sense within you that you are not as connected as you'd like to be when you pseudo listen.

If you're stuck in a cycle of pseudo listening, you may fool yourself into thinking that you're doing your best to listen while your partner is not. You may start to think, "Well, I'm listening, but my partner definitely isn't listening to me because they definitely don't get what I'm saying and barely pay attention." Look within and decide if maybe you're not listening as much as you could be either. Usually, when partners don't listen to one another, both partners need to work harder to listen. You may just be pseudo listening when you think you are listening genuinely. Genuine listeners know that pseudo listening can feign authentic listening, so carefully analyze whether you're really listening or not.

Pseudo listening will create more anxiety rather than solving it. Listening is something that most people think they know how to do, but many people fail to listen to beloved people in their lives. It can be hard to listen when you feel defensive or anxious, but it is a necessary step in relieving your relationship anxiety. If you're not able to listen, there's no way that your relationship will ever be secure enough to feel stress-free. You'll constantly worry about what your partner isn't saying, and the disconnect in your relationship will become bigger and more anxiety-inducing. Don't let your relationship deteriorate merely because you refuse to open your ears! Learn how to apply active listening to your life.

How to Listen

Step 1: Reflecting

When you actively listen, you cannot know if you understand the other person correctly unless you take an effort to reflect and double-check that your understanding is correct. You don't want to try to push your own agenda onto what the other person is thinking; however, you do need to communicate what the other person is saying in your own words to ensure that your conversation is going in the right direction. The more you practice this technique, the easier it will be to do in a conversation. Start slow and make small statements to reflect what the other person is saying when you talk to them.

As you reflect, you can use two techniques, mirroring, and paraphrasing. Mirroring is an easy method. It is repeating nearly precisely what the other person has said and reflecting it back to them. Paraphrasing, meanwhile, is crucial because it takes your communication to the next level and adds some degree of analysis to your reflection. You still reflect what the other person is saying, but you also show the other person you are trying to understand what they are saying. You're overcoming your own expectations and trying to look at things through the other person's perspective. You can successfully use either or both techniques, but note that paraphrasing usually takes your conversation to a deeper level and promotes more understanding.

Don't just reflect the content that the other person is saying, but you should also reflect the emotional connotations of what they are saying. There's a lot more to communication than what someone says. There are so many ways people express themselves to others, and you need to pay attention to more than just what someone is speaking. Pay attention to how they communicate, the faces they make, and the emotion in their voice. See if their shoulders are tense or if they look close to tears. Use all your senses to figure out what they are trying to express. If you limit your communication to just one sense, you'll not ever listen fully.

Try not to put words in the other person's mouth but express what you think they are saying. While you should try to observe multiple senses, do not overanalyze. Do not make assumptions that fit your narrative and that you can force their reactions to work how you'd like them to. Try to be as objective as you can, which no doubt is hard, and don't try to reflect until you are sure that you at least basically understand what they are saying. Remember, that even after you have practiced other steps in this process, you can always return to reflection and start the progression again to reorient yourself and get back on track with your communication.

As you practice reflection, you find how helpful it is for establishing strong communication. When you reflect on how someone is feeling, you stop making the conversation about yourself, and you emphasize the discussion onto your partner, allowing your communication to develop more organically and less solipsistically.

Step 2: Clarifying

Clarification is a step you need to take if you are struggling to understand hat your partner is saying. Clarification is the response to failed reflection. When you haven't managed to reflect what your partner is saying, or you have managed but you still don't fully understand the situation, you can turn to clarification. Clarification allows you to prod your partner with questions or prompts that can help you fill in the gaps, but this process is not meant to stop listening. You need to continue to listen to your partner. Be careful not to use clarification to shift the conversation to yourself. Clarification should still be about your partner and learning to understand them!

You can start by telling your partner that you aren't sure what they mean. Explain what parts of what they were saying that didn't resonate with you and that you can't understand. Don't be hostile or make them feel bad when you try to clarify, but say something like, "I'm starting to see what you're saying, but when you say ___ I'm not quite sure what you mean, so maybe you can clarify that part a bit so that I can understand better." Show them that even if you aren't clicking with what they are saying that you are still putting the effort in and want to be an active part of the conversation.

You can also ask your partner to repeat what they said so that you can understand it better. Again, do so in a cordial way, but give them the chance to rephrase what they were saying in a new way that may make more sense to you. Being a good communicator doesn't always mean that you can perfectly express yourself or understand someone else. To be a good communicator is to know how to navigate the hardships of communication. It is knowing that even when you're unsure, you can continue to converse and engage in the conversation without alienating the other person.

You can ask them to elaborate and give you examples of what you mean. Maybe you get the gist of what they are saying, but you want them to provide you with a few more examples so that you can understand the more nuanced parts o your partner's statements. Elaboration is a great way to give a person a chance to talk more and to explore their ideas deeper. Your partner may not have even realized that they needed to say more until you encouraged them to say more and dive deeper into their feelings. In your listening process, your partner becomes more engaged with you, and they become more aware of their emotions, which is great for your relationship.

Finally, if you're still not clear, you can ask questions, but you should be sure that your questions are open-ended and allow your partner to express themselves without your judgment or limitations. Questions should never feel aggressive, like a coup of the conversation. They should promote your listening experience. You'll eventually get to be the talker, but you need to focus on listening for now.

Step 3: Feedback, Expressing Your Needs, Validation

The third-step of listening is you acting on what you have heard. Now, it is your time to start taking the listening and putting it into action. You may need to go back to the listening steps soon, but now is the part of the conversation that includes your more understanding input and some of your own perspective. Remember that you still don't want to steamroll what your partner was saying, but you can be more upfront about how you feel and your responses in this step. During this step, many people get carried away and become overly passionate about expressing everything they're feeling, and doing so invalidates what they said, so be careful with how you approach speaking.

Once you are sure to have reflected and clarified what our partner has said, you can give your own feedback. Be sure not to make your input pushy or judgmental, but still show your perspective. Let's say that your discussing finances. You want to spend money on a new car, and your partner wants to save for a house. You could say, "I understand that you want to save for a new house, and I can see why that would be a good idea because we're thinking of having a kid soon, but my current car is unreliable. I'm worried about having to drive long distances to work in it with my safety." Your concerns are valid, and so are your partner's in this scenario, which is how you show that you have listened while being true to yourself.

Show an understanding of your partner's needs, but you also need to express yours. Your partner should be listening to you now. Continue to reflect what you heard your partner say while adding in your own perspective. You can't just drop the information that you gathered when you were listening. You have to maintain hints to your partner's perspective in your perspective. Working together means that you have to learn to share perspectives and make compromises based on your individual points of views. You can find ways to meet each other halfway and breakthrough any miscommunication issues.

Throughout the process, validate whatever your partner has said. When your partner makes other comments, even as you are speaking your part, be sure to pay attention to what they are saying. Don't go on a tirade about how they are wrong. Say, "You gave your perspective, and now I'm giving mine, which is different, but it's not better or worse." You don't want to emphasize that your view is somehow superior. You'll likely think your view is superior, but that is not a reason to make your partner feel invalidated. Good communication means making everyone feel like they have a place at the table to speak and be heard.

Listening is a two-way street, and it mostly requires you to sit back, turn off your judgments, and encourage your partner to speak, but in the final step, you have to learn to talk while still absorbing what your partner has said.

CHAPTER 8

How to Cultivate Self-Love

You know how vital self-compassion is if you want your relationship to be strong, but beyond just self-compassion, the act of being understanding to ourselves, we need also to love ourselves. You need to be more than just compassionate to yourself. You need to embrace who you are completely before you can expect that anyone else will accept you in the way you want to be accepted. If you can love yourself, your partner can love you even more deeply than they already do.

Practice Generosity

Generosity allows you to show love to the world, and when you show love to the world, you show love to yourself because you are part of this world. When you become disconnected from things larger than yourself, it's easy to lose sight of generosity. You become so fixated on aspects of yourself that you can't seem to love, that you lose track of all the fantastic opportunities there are to do good in the world and make it a better place. Generosity is connected to gratitude because you learn to be thankful for what you have and give some of what you have to others when you generous. In turn, gratitude helps you focus on the positives rather than the negatives, which reduces your anxiety.

Volunteer your time with organizations or people that fill you with passion. Find organizations that make you feel alive and help them. Maybe they help people with something that you have experienced or someone close to you has experiences, or maybe they just do really good work and give back in a way that makes you excited. Whatever the case, you should feel motivated to help certain causes. Don't sit on your butt and squander that passion. Use it as much as you can. Even just a little time given to other people, such as an elderly neighbor, can change your life and other people's lives as well.

Learn to give to your partner. Making some sacrifices can be rewarding. You don't need to be a martyr, but allowing your partner to have what they want sometimes without a big fight is how a relationship should work. While sometimes it can be hard to give in because of stubbornness, if you actually don't care that much, don't put up an argument because you want to argue for the sake of mere argument! You can say, "Yeah, I think that's a great idea," even if you're apathetic about the actual. It is generous to appreciate what your partner wants when you can do so without sacrificing much because little acts like keeping the relationship running smoothly.

Be generous at least once a day. You don't have to give a thousand dollars to charity each day, but you should find something that utilizes your giving spirit. Generosity can be anything that spreads goodwill and kindness to others, so you don't have to stress. If you go through life with a generous spirit and open to giving to others, you will be giving at least once a day without even having to exert thought. Through this process, you will find joy and fulfillment because it is good to see parts of the universe more significant than yourself and give good vibes into those parts of life. You'll become more assured in yourself. When you do good acts, it's a whole lot easier to feel proud of yourself.

Small acts can go a long way. What starts as just a basic acts become a huge part of your life. Your small acts of generosity may not seem like much at first, but as you consistently complete them, you will start to feel more secure in yourself. Generosity alone cannot create self-love, but it is a great starting point because it helps you emerge from your negative self-talk and focus on the amazing things you do with your body and mind. Tiny acts have a massive impact on the world and your outlook on that world.

Spend time with people who need help. When people in your life need your help, don't avoid them. Take the time to help them instead. Don't let them take advantage of you, but being there for people and helping them with your skills is a great way to find a world connection and to become part of something. Volunteering once at a soup kitchen can be rewarding, but getting to know the faces in that soup kitchen as you continue to volunteer there creates connection and additional meaning. When you have that meaning in your life, you start to see yourself in new ways, and you become more open to how other people can help you in unexpected ways. You start to understand that it's normal to need help and generosity sometimes, just as it is normal to give it.

Give the world what you want to get back. Make intentional choices about what you give because what you put into the world, you get back. If you put kindness and love into the world, you will get kindness and love back, and those aspects will start to become a greater part of you, but if you give the world your negativity, you will feel worse about yourself as negative energies seem to fly at you. Your perspective shapes what opportunities you see, and when you can only see things that will go wrong, you miss out on what can go right.

Generosity helps you become more aware of your gifts. You can learn to be thankful for what you have. You stop begrudging the universe for what you don't have, and you embrace everything you have been blessed with. When you are generous, you can use your skills to the fullest. Sometimes, we're stuck with jobs that we don't like and don't use our gifts in ways that don't fulfill us, but when we are generous, we can fill that gap and use our blessing in ways that make us feel how we have longed to feel for so long.

Additionally, when you are generous, you stop thinking so much about yourself and increase empathy. Empathy is one of the most important qualities that ou can carry into a relationship, so when you build it up through generosity, you bring that empathy home with you. You can be more generous with your partner. You can learn to see life from the perspectives of people who are nothing like you. You can see that they are worthy of life and respect because they are humans, regardless of their differences.

Generous people have the open minds and the open hearts they need to treat themselves better. When you treat other people better, you are more likely to treat yourself better too.

Treat Yourself With Kindness

Give yourself a break when things get hard in life. When your relationship, job, and family life all seem to be collapsing in on you, don't start beating yourself up over everything you could have done differently. It doesn't benefit you to be inflexible with yourself, and it doesn't help to keep pushing through all the negative feelings you have with no respect for what you are feeling. What you need to do is treat yourself with more kindness. If you cannot be kind to yourself, your relationships will always be more challenging because you'll struggle against yourself.

Don't expect to be perfect. You're never going to do everything right, so quit trying. Put the pressure away and let yourself exist without intense expectations. Take a breath and remember that it's okay to mess up sometimes. It's okay to do things that you regret and have to apologize for them. Everyone makes mistakes at work, with their kids, or in any other sphere of their life. Don't let those mistakes make your relationship work. There's no use trying to convince your partner you're perfect because you acting perfectly doesn't allow you to be vulnerable.

Don't deprive yourself. You deserve to have things you like in your life. If you like a guilty-pleasure TV show, watch it. If you like a high-calorie chocolate bar as a snack, eat it! While there's always room for moderation in life, sometimes, it's good to indulge. You can't say, "I'm never going to watch that show again because it isn't intellectual." Not everything has to be intellectual. Don't hold yourself to such high standards that you can no longer enjoy things that are deemed "lesser" by society. If you like something and it doesn't hurt other people, there's no reason not to do it!

Eat a balanced diet. When you eat a balanced diet, you show your body and mind kindness. Don't restrict certain "unhealthy" foods, but try to eat more foods that are nutritionally dense like whole grains, legumes, fruits, and vegetables rather than nutritionally empty foods like junk foods and sweets. Eating balanced meals makes your brain more balanced because it is filled with better fuel. Additionally, nutrients ensure that your bodily functions all remain in order. Without balance, your skin, vision, and a myriad of other parts of your body worsen, which can lead to insecurity and pain that makes it harder to have a clear head and engage in relationships. If your body doesn't feel good, you will never feel good about yourself.

Get more active. You don't have to go to the gym and start intense workouts, but if you can spend a few more minutes per day being active, such as taking a walk, your body and mind will feel better. Activity sends endorphins through your body, which are feel-good chemicals that boost your mood. Exercise can also help you sleep better.

Thus, staying active can significantly improve how you feel.

When you take a few steps to treat yourself with kindness, your life gets a whole lot better. By being just slightly kinder to yourself, your life will change forever, and you'll be in the mindset to make better decisions about your relationship.

Know Who You

If you want to love yourself, you have to know yourself, which can be hard if challenging life incidents have fragmented your sense of self or you've gotten lost in your relationship.

Your past doesn't have to define you. Whatever has happened in your past, it doesn't have to define you now. You get to define yourself, and you can define yourself in whatever ways you want. If you were emotionally distant in the past, you don't have to be emotionally distant in the present. You can become who you want. Certain fundamental parts of yourself cannot change, but you can shape what those parts mean to you as a whole person.

Embrace parts of yourself that you keep hidden. Stop running away from the things that you like. Maybe you secretly like to watch action movies even though your partner always says they are stupid. Stop keeping your love a secret. Embrace your love for action movies, even if your partner doesn't understand why you love them. You shouldn't feel ashamed about having individual interests because while you have to put some of your individuality aside in relationships, your characteristics don't go away the second you have a significant other. You still have your identity; however, you interact with it in different ways. You get to determine how you interact with your uniqueness and let me tell you, hiding your interests never works.

You're exactly how you're meant to be. Nothing needs to change about you because you're exactly how you should be. You don't need to change your hair, your sense of style, or any other part of your identity to be a worthy partner. If your partner cannot appreciate you as you inherently are, they will never truly love you, and your relationship will always have anxiety. Chances are that your partner loves your quirks and that the insecurities you have are because of past experiences and doubts you've experienced more than your partner. Usually, unless you're in a toxic relationship, your insecurities are fueled b miscommunication, but self-esteem issues create them. You may be an overall confident person, but in certain areas, your self-esteem may still suffer.

Try to do better, but don't try to change yourself. It's one thing to want to make better decisions and improve yourself, but it is another thing altogether to try to change yourself completely. Aim to be the best version of yourself. When you get up each morning, vow to act in the best way that you can, even though you'll never get it all right. You cannot change things like your personality, your sexuality, or your genetic tendencies, but you can learn to embrace them and handle them in ways that make you happiest and confident.

Don't let your partner define who you are. Your partner is an integral part of your life, but you are so much more than what they say you are. Even if they say only good things about you, it can feel stifling to have your partner define you, so start defining yourself.

Honor Parts of Yourself You Hate

Think about the part of yourself that fills you with the most hate. These are the things that make you want to crawl up and hide from the world. They make you feel shame, and you've probably begged God, or whatever greater power you believe in, that something could change those things about yourself. You let those parts fill you with insecurity and anxiety, even though those parts of yourself aren't usually as treacherous as you fear. What you see as bad may be something that other people see as good, and those parts of yourself undoubtedly are the ones that set you apart from other people. In a society that often encourages conformity, it can be hard to be different, but your differences should make you proud.

If you're thinking of a physical feature that you hate about yourself, think of how that changes how you interact with the world. Does it make it harder to do certain things? If it does, think of the ways you can overcome that challenge. Remind yourself that there are still ways you can accomplish your goals. Alternatively, you can reshape your goals to fit the needs of your body. If your bodily insecurities don't prohibit you from doing what you want to do, there's no reason for hating that part of you. If your nose still works but it is slightly crooked, it only hurts you to hate that part of yourself. Remember, focus on what your body can do, not how it looks.

If you're thinking about an emotional part of yourself that you dread, figure out why you villainize that part of you. What is it about specific traits, such as sentimentality, that make you feel like less of a person? Maybe you're naturally emotionally sensitive, and people have made fun of you for being quick to tear up. Your sensitivity doesn't make you weak or childish. It is a part of you. It shows your ability to have compassion and feel life more deeply than others. What other people call your weaknesses are things that you can turn into strengths. Use your sensitivity to help people and be more empathetic in your relationship. Whatever it is that you don't like, there's a way to make the best of it.

There are so many parts that people usually hate about themselves, and you don't have to like those parts of yourself quite yet, but you do need to make peace with them. There are some things you'll learn to like—like your crooked nose—but there are certain parts of yourself that you'll probably always dislike, but if you can learn not to turn your dislike of parts of yourself into hate for all of yourself, you'll be better off. Try to love yourself, even the worst parts of yourself, because that's the way you'll feel more confident and secure. Some features of you will never change, and those parts of you shouldn't be ones that you try to change or feel guilty for having. If you can't change it, don't lose sleep over it.

Learn to Love Flaws

It's time to learn how to love your flaws, or at least tolerate them. When you open your mind to loving parts of yourself that you've avoided, you'll feel more prone to vulnerability, and you'll have more confidence.

Start using flaws as advantages. Maybe people have called you bossy, and you feel wrong for being so bossy. Change the language of your flaws and begin to realize that, maybe, you're "assertive" instead. Changing the language of your flaws is a great way to find a silver lining. If you're timid, you may feel like a scared mouse, but contemplative is a much better descriptor. Traits you have can always be used in both a good and a bad way, so choose the good way, and as you act on your personality, start to look at the good way to use qualities you have deemed "flaws."

Find ways to overcome your limitations. If you have limits, don't let them stop you. Use them as fuel to do better. Everyone has things they think they cannot do, often because people tell them that they cannot, but you can never know that you cannot do something. The biggest reason you cannot do something is that you do not try. There will always be limitations, but you can usually shrink your limits and expand your boundaries with some effort. You may not always get what you want when you set out to break your limits, but you will always be rewarded for pushing through. Sometimes, life surprises you, but surprises are often fun.

Don't let other people use your flaws against you. Never let people weaponize your flaws to make you feel worse about yourself or to poke holes in your relationship. Resist the negative energies that people try to spread to you and show that you are self-assured. You don't need other people telling you to be ashamed. There's enough shame in the world as it is, and shame only makes relationships harder.

While there are many qualities you don't want to have, you need to love even the ones that are hard to love being. Doing so will teach you how to love other flawed people in the same way. Things you don't like are what you unique, so embrace all those parts of yourself. When you love yourself, other people will love you as well, and they will be able to communicate better with you and in new ways.

Steps to Being in Love with Yourself

You need to start finding ways to love yourself more. Explore all the opportunities you have to love yourself and find activities that fill you with more respect. Choose to do things that make you feel better about yourself, and continue to practice those things. Don't waste time developing skills that don't make you feel fulfilled. Take your passion and let that passion guide you because that passion is your personality, giving you hints about what it wants. Your passion is not always logical, but it shows you your dreams, and it gives you the chance to get to know yourself better.

Your relationship with other people hinges on your relationship with yourself. Until you address any lingering self-hate that you have, you're always going to feel insecure. It doesn't matter how good your relationship is. If you have insecurities that you haven't addressed, you're always going to fear that your partner will wake up one day and realize that you aren't good enough. You'll desperately cling onto your relationship, terrified that your partner will stop loving you or leave you alone. Those fears create cracks in relationships, which is why you need to understand your individual insecurities before you can say goodbye to your relationship anxiety.

Think of your inner child when things get hard. When you start to yourself, think about yourself as a five-year-old. This child is always somewhere within you, influencing how you behave, but take the time to consider this child before you insult yourself. Does that child deserve that kind of treatment? Would you want your little self to be treated like you treat an adult you? If the answer is no, you need to reevaluate your relationship with yourself. Treat yourself with the tenderness and love that your five-year-old self deserves (and maybe didn't get from other people). You deserve dignity. You always have, and you always will.

Go into the world being a person you can be proud to know. When you make decisions, make ones that you would like to see your best friend make. If you would be disappointed by a particular choice from someone you loved, it may be a wrong choice for you to make. If something would make you feel shame, address whether that shame is connected to morality or societal expectations. If it's related to societal expectations, you may be shaming yourself for things out of your control, but if an action goes against your morals, then even if it would please your partner, it's not respectful to yourself.

Take breaks when you need them. Everyone needs moments to recharge and reorient their connection with themselves. Take those moments as much as you need them. Don't be ashamed of needing to do certain things for your own well-being. Your partner doesn't have the right to your time and attention 24/7. Sometimes, you need to go out with your friends on your own, or you need to have time alone in your room to relax without interruption. Communicate these needs with your partner, but don't think that you need to explain your choices because it's your right to use your time as you choose. Your choices do influence your relationship, so keep that in mind, but they are still yours to make.

Indulge in little acts of self-care. Painting your nails, going for a run, or taking a hot bath are a few examples of activities that people use to restore themselves. These activities are just a few of the things you can do to show yourself that you want to take care of your body and your mind, but they are great because they are things you can do that are dedicated to showing yourself respect and compassion. Things that seem vain can often be meditative and help you express yourself— like painting nails. These acts shouldn't be done to fit societal standards, but they are excellent for making you feel more connected to yourself.

Don't accept disrespect from anyone. People don't have the right to disparage you, and you should be honest when they make you feel disrespected. Sometimes, they won't even realize that what they are saying is offensive and demeaning. You deserve to be treated with dignity, and you should expect that in both your relationship and your other interactions with people. When you expect dignity, even if you don't get it, you ensure yourself of your worth.

You are a complete person right now. You don't need a person or a complete personality change to be a fuller person. You are full now, and you have always been full. Don't feel the need to be someone else or change you are to fit your idea of what it means to be a person. Trying to be someone else will only make you more insecure, and your partner will sense that you're not genuine. People who love you want to see the real you. They want you to feel content in who you are, and you no doubt want that for yourself as well. Don't fool yourself into wanting to be someone else because when you do that, you're in for a lot of stress.

If your partner wants to change you, no amount of coping tools and anxiety-reducing techniques can save your relationship. Love yourself today because there's no reason to keep putting self-love off.

CHAPTER 9

Light Up Your Love Life

Don't let your love light go dark just because you're busy or you've been in love for years. You can never neglect the anxious side of your love life because if you neglect that part of your life, you will start to feel a disconnect, and you will wonder if your relationship is worth all the effort. Learn to take comfort in your relationship rather than wanting to run away from it.

How Anxiety Dulls Relationships

The more you let anxiety linger, the more it will dull your relationship. As you're probably aware, relationships aren't just harmed by anxiety, but they are dulled by it. They are aged before their time, and they become less vibrant under the stresses of trying to alleviate the anxiety in unhealthy manners. When your relationship is driven by anxiety, all the things that make your relationship so impressive start to fade into the background. You lose your hopes of a future together, and as you scramble to put the pieces together, you feel overwhelmed by all the things that have become muted by your anxiety.

It makes you less passionate. When you're anxious about your relationship, your passion is among the first things to go. Many couples with well-established relationships become so part of each other's lives that they get used to the status quo, and they aren't used to how the relationship changes. They often have children, pets, jobs, or other responsibilities that keep them busy, and with all the hecticness, they forget that sometimes they need romantic moments to keep their relationship vibrant. Cody and Olivia had three little kids, and they didn't notice that they had lost track of each other until it was nearly too late. They went from the perfect little family to fighting with each other all the time. When they began to have once-weekly date nights after dropping the kids with Olivia's niece, they began to mend the rift that had popped up between them.

Anxiety hides your love under layers of bitterness. It shows you what could be wrong rather than what it is right. It takes well-intentioned gestures, and it turns into scary gestures that can even feel like threats! Partners can try to do what they think each other wants, but in the process, only increase the insecurity that their partner feels. It can feel impossible to please a loved one with anxiety, and it can push relationships to their limits. Anxiety limits your ability to see the vibrancy of the life you have with your partner, and your partner may feel that they are failing you no matter what they do, which is a recipe for relationship disaster.

Anxiety makes it hard for the non-anxious partner to understand what is happening. If one partner has never been anxious about a relationship, they're going to struggle to know how to help. They'll try to reassure you, but they won't know how unless they try to get to the root of the anxiety. Even the most empathetic partner may not know how to react to their partner's anxiety because anxiety is sensitive. What appeases it one day won't necessarily appease it the next. The unpredictability of anxiety makes it even more of a monster, but once you understand the patterns, it's easier to see how it impacts people.

When you are anxious, you cannot focus on the things that make you most happy. You get lost in all the things that make you miserable. The hardships of your relationship replay in a loop in your head, and you wonder how you are ever going to rise above them. You don't think that you'll ever feel better about your relationship. It seems like you're never going to feel secure, which's a hard feeling to face. It makes waking up and having to deal with your relationship a struggle rather than a delight. Your shoulders feel heavy with the weight of something that should make you feel good.

Anxiety makes communication more of a challenge. As anxiety progresses, communication doesn't become easier. All the feelings that are building within you become a wall that separates you from your voice. You lose yourself in the anxiety, not just your relationship. You become a muted form of yourself because you cannot say what you want to say, no matter how hard you try. Communication feels too hard, even though it will be the things that redeems you from your misery. Your anxiety spreads into your normal life too. It becomes intrusive in any relationship you have, not just your romantic one.

When someone is anxious, a relationship always becomes more divisive. It's normal to start fighting when you're in an anxious relationship, and you start fighting about things that seem so silly. One couple, Lydia and Arman, used to practically never fight, but then after an accident that caused Arman's face to be deformed, Arman became worried that Lydia could never love him because he no longer felt handsome. The more Lydia insisted that Arman was just as handsome to her as ever, the more Arman became insecure. Anytime Lydia would tell Arman how much she loved him, he would lash out and feel like she was pitying him. Lydia was honest, but their lack of communication about Arman's sense of self-worth and fears after the accident made a normally tranquil couple start having arguments all the time. As Arman worked through his issues, and Lydia tried to understand his hangups, they began to cool down their fiery arguments. While they're still mending their relationship, they are on a path towards reparation.

You forget how you make each other happy. As you become focused on yourself as anxiety strikes, it becomes hard to make your partner happy because you're so concentrated on your unhappiness. Lydia and Arman also faced this issue; he didn't notice how hard Lydia was working on trying to make Arman happy because he was sure that she was putting on a front. For her part, Lydia didn't notice what a hard time Arman was having because he acted like he was fine most of the time. Their story shows that communication causes unhappiness in couples.

You cannot have faith in your relationship when you have anxiety. You'll start to see doubt everywhere. You'll think that your partner is unhonest or that they aren't confiding in you enough. You'll start to worry about infidelity and inattentiveness. You might think that your partner's job is more important than you, or you may think that they're spending too much time with your best friend. Your emotions will go wild, even if your partner's behavior has nothing to do with their commitment to you. They may be seeing their friend more because they're seeking advice about what to do about their relationship or they need a distraction from the hard day to day drudgery of saving a failing relationship.

When you have relationship anxiety, everything becomes about individuals, not partnerships. You start to live your lives separately. You may sleep in the same bed, but you stick to your sides, and you never cross the invisible line that separates you form your partner. You become wary of one another, and your partner's normal activities like eating breakfast may spark anxiety. That's no way to live, and it's pretty demoralizing, and it's especially harmful if you have children who will pick up on your fragmented vibes. When you have children, you have to pay special attention to be kind to your partner, even if you don't think you'll be able to continue your relationship with them because tension can lead to children having relationship anxiety when they grow up.

It makes people feel unable to speak genuinely and to be themselves. Anxiety causes your personality to fade into the back as you try to fight to exist with your partner. You may be willing to sacrifice who you are just to cling onto your relationship, and while your intentions are good, it doesn't help anyone to pretend to be someone you're not, and it never truly fixes your issues. It keeps them going steadily into the future. You can ignore issues for a while with pretending, and you can delay their impact, but you cannot make them go away. They will linger and haunt you until you face them, or they destroy your relationship.

Anxiety is like taking a black and white picture of your relationship. Its details are lost in the picture. The more you let it linger, the less color there is in your relationship. Don't let your relationship become snapshots of once happy times. You deserve better than that. You deserve to live in the moment of your relationship and to appreciate all the colors that surround and fill your relationship with life and vibrancy. Anxiety numbs your relationship, and it makes it hard for partners to feel one another's presence, even when they're going through the motions of being a couple. Stop going through the motions as the colors fade to black and start living in color. There are colors all around you. All you have to do is embrace them, even when they're blindingly bright.

How Do I Help My Partner with Anxiety

If you're trying to help an anxious partner, it can be hard to know what to do, especially if you experience little anxiety yourself. You'll feel out of your element, but it is essential to know how to handle your anxious partner in ways that aren't dismissive and make your partner part of the process. Trying to do all the work yourself will never work. As lovely as it would be to fix your partner's anxiety, all you can do is be supportive. With practice and a few of these techniques, you'll have some insight into how to deal with an anxious partner. Be the support system that your partner needs, and don't try to force them to do anything that they don't want to do because trying to force someone to do something often makes the situation worse because it makes them feel like they are out of control.

When They Lash Out, Show You Care

When your partner lashes out, instead of getting angry back, learn to show that you care. Show compassion for them, even when you are feeling defensive. When you feel defensive, it's usually time to evaluate why. It's time to look within yourself and see why you feel so attacked and to evaluate why your partner may be trying to hurt you. Often, it will be an attempt to push you away to try to protect themselves. The rational knowledge of what is happening won't make you feel less hurt, but it can help you calm down and try to handle the situation in a way that won't lead to escalation. The last thing you want to do is make the problem more explosive and say things in anger that you cannot take back and only serve to make your partner's anxiety worse.

If your insecure partner knows that you care for them, they can better fight their anxiety even when they are at their lowest. When you reiterate your care daily, you will feed your partner's unconscious mind reassuring messages. Much of the anxiety stems from the unconscious brain, so giving their unsconscious brain new messages can start to be less secure without even being consciously aware of the changes happening. Of course, becoming conscious of unconscious thoughts is essential when the time is right, but not everything you do has to be a deep psychological dive. That would be exhausting, so give little messages of care whenever you can to make the journey a little easier on both of you.

It is hard to keep your emotions under check, but for the good of your relationship, sometimes, you must. Until your relationship gets better, you're going to need to try to keep your emotions in check and be calm with your partner. There will be times when you'll lash out, and you may have anxiety yourself, which makes it hard for you to control your emotions, but both of you need to try to resist lashing out whenever possible to promote a sense of security in your relationship. When you can keep arguments in calm tones, each partner is less likely to get upset and say cruel, anxiety-driven statements. When a partner doubts your love, you need to show them that you will be there for them no matter what.

Take meditative breaths before you let your emotions carry you away. If you're struggling to manage your emotions, it helps to take some breaths before you let yourself speak. Get in the habit of taking ten seconds of breathing to let the initial surge of emotion you have calm before you say something on impulse. This breathing-time reminds you to think about your actions, and sometimes, you'll have an outburst regardless, but in many instances, this method conditions you to become less reactive the more you practice it. Your partner could probably benefit from this method as well because it's good for anyone who finds themselves reacting emotionally (which is everyone at times if we're honest with ourselves).

It's okay if you lash out sometimes. It's human to lash out, but you need to try to be as caring as you can. Lashing out doesn't mean that you can go on with your day like nothing happened or ignore the words you said. You need to apologize if you said something that you didn't mean, and you need to explain to your partner how you were in the wrong. You don't have to take total blame, but you need to acknowledge things that you did wrong in the situation. Admitting your wrongs takes some of the pressure off your partner, and it makes you both responsible for an argument that you both participated in, which connects you. It's easier to deal with your actions when you can share the responsibility with your partner. It's rare to have just one partner who did something wrong, so when you both take your blame with grace, it makes a huge difference.

Even if you don't understand the situation, care is still essential. You can never treat your partner like they are unimportant to you or that you don't care about what happens to them. If you treat them that way, their insecurities will only increase as will your relationship's rift. Everyone wants to be important to their partners, so be patient with your partner and show them that you will care for them as long as you can. Make them feel like you would never leave them, even as they try to push you away. The proof is in your actions more than your words.

Help Them Confront Their Fears

Don't let your partner get away with giving in to their fears. When you think they are being fearful rather than trusting your relationship, call them out on it. Say something like, "Hey, I know what you're feeling is probably intense, and I can understand why you would feel that way, but I think you are using your fears as an excuse to avoid some of our issues that we need to address. I want to make this conversation a safe space for you, but we cannot have a conversation at all if you let your anxiety win." Sometimes, they won't take well to your explanation, but for some people, that can give them the reassurance they need to move forward with whatever you both need to do. You know your partner well, so find techniques that work for them. Hold them accountable while still considering how they must feel.

Jade and Julie were married for one year when Jade's worry that Julie would leave her became all-consuming when Julie got a promotion and had to work more. Jade was reminded of her work-obsessed father, who would always spend too long at work, and then, eventually left the family altogether. Julie feared that there was nothing she could do to soothe Jade's fears, but then she learned to challenge those fears, which allowed Jade to face her demons and become more communicative.

Hold their hand as they face their fears. Sometimes, your reassurances aren't going to make their fears less profound. You won't be able to vanquish all your partner's fears, but you can hold their hand and be there for them as they deal with their anxiety. Sometimes, being there is the best thing a person can do for another person. Talking doesn't always help, but knowing that someone will be by your side, feels profound. In fact, it is a way of listening. It is hearing your partner's pain and listening to it. You absorb their pain, even if you cannot change it.

Be a source of reason for them when they need it. People with anxiety sometimes want someone to remind them that they are not being logical. They want to hear the logical side of things because it can help them put things back into perspective. Again, you'll have to experiment and see what your partner needs for their anxiety, but the reminder that "Your anxiety is real, but the messages that it is telling you are overblown or completely false" can be a good starting point. We all need reminders sometimes, so you can help remind your partner that anxiety is not a tangible thing. It is an abstract idea that causes reality to look bleaker.

Help them understand that you want what is best for them. Don't just tell them that, but show them that you want to do whatever you can to help them through their anxiety. Do not be condescending or act like you know better than they do, but do show your partner that you will put their needs first. Act in ways that prove that you will put them above yourself some of the time, and that you will support in whatever they decide they need to improve their anxiety. Make them feel as though you are a willing participant in the process and make sure they don't feel like they are a burden to you because too often people feel like they are burdening their partners with their anxiety.

Know that fears don't go away overnight. No matter how great of a conversation you have with your partner, their worries won't vanish after one heart to heart. Some reassurances aren't enough to get rid of fears forever, and even years after the anxiety is mostly gone, it can still pop up from time to time. Moreover, recovery from relationship anxiety isn't linear. There will be ups and downs. Sometimes, you'll go two steps forward, but other times, you'll go one step back. Overall, you'll make progress if you continue pushing through the anxiety with your partner, but it isn't as easy as it may seem from the outside.

Fears are hard to beat, but it is easier to beat them when you have help, which is why partners, whether they have anxiety themselves or not, need to take an active role in their loved one's recovery process. It shouldn't feel like a burden to help your partner work through their issues just as it shouldn't feel like a burden to your partner to help you through your problems. Partners are meant to work together, and when you battle giant monsters like anxiety, your relationship becomes stronger. You learn to relate to one another in new and exciting ways. Further, you learn new things about your partner and yourself in the process, which is always a wonderful thing.

Know They Might Try to Push You Away

When anxiety is in the picture, it is easy to self-sabotage and try to push your partner away. They may feel uncomfortable when you try to get involved in curing your relationship by their side. They may say, "This is my problem, and I need to handle it alone," but it is a problem for both of you when it leads to issues between you, so you need to resist the barriers they put up to keep you out. Urge your partner to let you into their life. You cannot force them to open up, but you can create an environment that makes them feel safe to open up and to share their worries.

When your partner pushes you away, it's often because they feel shame that keeps them from being open with you. They don't want you to see how "messed up" they are, or they're afraid that if they show you that they are insecure that you will think they're pathetic or weak. One young woman, Jenny, had an eating disorder for years before she married Jarome. Her eating disorder was cured for the most part, but she still had some insecurities about her weight and body that lingered, and she had never admitted them to Jarome. She would get upset a lot before they went out as she tried to find something to wear, but every time Jarome tried to console her, she would push him away. Finally, she let him in, and he finally learned more about the worries she had. She would think she was too fat to be loved or that her husband only loved her if she looked pretty. She knew these fears were irrational and that Jarome wasn't like that, but the thoughts lingered anyway. They got better when Jarome could address them properly and knew how not to trigger Jenny so much.

Your partner disconnecting is not personal. When your partner distances themselves from you, they are not doing it to hurt you most of the time. Usually, it is a method they use to protect themselves from rejection. Fearful people tend to self-sabotage because it's easier to be the cause of the relationship's destruction than to worry that the relationship could potentially fall apart because there was something inherently wrong with them. For example, Jenny tried to hide her weight and food issues because she didn't want Jarome to think that she was broken. She pushed her husband away so that he wouldn't reject her when he learned more about her. Her fears were self-sabotaging because their relationship was hurt by Jenny pushing Jarome away, not the things that made Jenny feel unworthy enough to push away from Jarome.

Pushing someone away is a response to fear, so don't feed into the fear and show them that you aren't going to let them run away. See if you can get them to stay and face their fear instead of letting them push away from you. When they try to push you away, make a commitment to get closer. Don't assume they are pushing away because they are bored of you or think something is wrong with you. Confront your partner and get to the bottom of their actions because it's better to have the truth than to wonder why your partner ran away when the relationship had been going so well.

It isn't easy to deal with a partner who is pushing you away, but if you can learn to do it, your relationship will become stronger. Prove that you want to be part of their fight against their anxiety.

Reassure Them That They are Safe

Anxiety is often caused by insecurity that leads to your partner feeling that your relationship isn't safe for them. You need to create a sense of security in any relationship you have, and both you and your partner should create that safe spae for each other, even when you're fighting.

Do not storm out when you are angry. Especially if your partner has abandonment issues, avoid storming out without any conversation because such behavior can feel like you're abandoning them, even if logically, they know you are not. You can need space when you're upset, but explain to them that you need space to deal with your feelings and that you'll be back once you have gotten some air and have processed your emotions. It keeps your partner's anxiety lower when you explain your actions, but it will probably not make it go away altogether. Never leave a room angry. Always talk in a calm tone before taking the space you need.

Never go too far into their personal space during any confrontation. When you make a partner feel crowded, they can feel unsafe, even if they trust you. When someone's personal space is invaded during an argument, they naturally feel anxious because of natural bodily responses that we all have, so be careful with getting too close to them too suddenly and not move aggressively to keep their fear levels in check. When you respect your partner's personal space, you show that you appreciate them as a person, and you avoid making them upset over nothing.

Making threats is never healthy. You should never threaten your partner, even if you think you're making harmless threats. Don't give ultimatums. Tell them how it is, but never say, "Do this or else." Your partner is an autonomous person, so they have the right to make their decisions without undue pressure from you.

Protect their feelings when you can. Do not try to shield them from the realities of the world, but do not say things in anger just because you want to hurt them. While doing so can feel good in the moment, it does not create a safe environment.

Remember Your Mental Health

Your mental health matters too. You may also have anxiety that you deal with, even if it is not to the extent of your partner's or is not even about your relationship. To help your partner, you have to keep yourself healthy and remember that your mental health is important, and when you have mental health issues, deal with those first for the sake of yourself and your relationship.

Don't do anything that's going to ruin your mental well-being. If your partner has expectations of you that you're not able to meet because of your mental health, be clear about why you need to be more flexible with what that expectation means to account for your needs. You should never martyr yourself to help your partner.

If you cannot deal with the situation alone, professional help may benefit you. Sometimes, you and your partner will have a lot of baggage to unpack, and that can often be done best with the help of a professional who, along with these tips, can lead you towards relationship security. Mental health professionals are best equipped to deal with the particularities of your situation.

It is good to want to help your partner, but you cannot do so at the expense of yourself, so take the time you need to deal with your own issues, and make sure your mental health is strong before you try to take on your partner's mental health issues.

Don't Assume

When you make assumptions, you close yourself off to listening and understanding what your partner is going through. You stop putting your partner first, and you try to make the situation easier on yourself. Assumptions are shortcuts that are good in many situations, but when dealing with your partner's anxiety and general concerns, they are often dismissive.

Remember the listening techniques in this book, and use them instead of getting frustrated with your partner. Listening helps you avoid the assumptions you will be tempted to make to get to quick answers. Know now that there are no quick answers or shortcuts to solving this problem. You must put in hard work with your partner.

You cannot read your partner's mind, so don't try. It doesn't help anyone to guess what is going on with your partner without discussing how they feel.

If you cannot fully understand your partner's insecurity, do not tell them that you think they are being foolish. No one likes to feel like their feelings are being dismissed or waved off as silly. There's nothing worse than sharing something you are worried about and then being laughed at and patted on the head like a little kid. Don't assume that because what your partner is feeling is irrational or fear-driven that it isn't real or that it isn't important. You're surely scared of things that others would call "silly," but those fears still feel true to you, and the same is true of your partner's concerns. It's one thing to approach the situation with an analytical lens, but never make someone feel stupid for their worries.

Assumptions can do more harm than good. When you make assumptions, you skip a vital stage in the communication process. You guess what the situation is without exploring that situation. What is happening on the outside is often very different from what is happening on the inside, so making an assumption is a disservice to your partner and your relationship. While you may know your partner incredibly well, there are so many things about them that you won't know. Their feelings may change rapidly, so just because they felt one way one day doesn't mean that they will feel the same the next. Be open to how dynamic emotions can be and embrace that in your handling of your partner's anxiety.

Love is Stronger Than Tumult

At the end of the day, the love between two people is stronger than the hardships they face if they choose to let that love continue to exist. Love cannot save a relationship all the time, but it can bridge many gaps. Show that you love when it would be easier to express negative feelings. Let your love remind you why you continue to fight for your partner. If you don't want your partner to feel safe and secure, you are not in love. Create a sense of security for your partner, and prove that you are devoted to helping your relationship get better from the anxiety that plagues it.

CHAPTER 10

Keep Your Relationship Flourishing

Once you have established a stronger, anxiety-free relationship, you need to maintain the changes you have made. You cannot revert to old habits and expect that you won't feel more anxiety. Relationships require upkeep, so take the necessary steps to keep your relationship flourishing.

Stay Engaged With Your Partner

You need to remain engaged with your partner long after you have gone through the steps of this book. An anxiety-free relationship requires you to maintain the healthy relationship tools that you have learned from this book, and some additional upkeep that will ensure you don't stray from making decisions that will keep you feeling connected to your relationship, yourself, and your partner. Even years after you've dealt with your anxiety, you'll still need to continue these practices or your anxiety will come flooding back. It does get easier to continue healthy engagement as you practice it more.

Check-in with each other. If something seems off with your partner, check in on them, and you don't need a reason to check in with them. Sometimes, it's nice to check in to show that you care for them and for the sake of wanting to know more about your partner. When you check in with each other, you keep your expectations in line, and you make sure that you don't lose track of one another's wants. You keep your mind flexible, and you allow the progression of your relationship to happen as it will rather than making a plan with no room for deviation. When you check-in, you can recalculate your journey when you realize that the path you're on won't take you where you want to go. This method is so much better than waiting until you keep going and don't realize things are wrong until they are catastrophically wrong.

Continue listening. Listening is something that you can do when it just serves you. You can't say, "I have heard what my partner has said, and I now I know them and will always know them as well as I do right now." That's not how people work. They evolve, and their situations change, so how they are feeling and what they are saying now is going to evolve just as your relationship does. You wouldn't want to be held to everything you said ten years ago. When you were a kid and said you wanted to be an astronaut for a living, no one is surprised when you evolve and decide you want to be something else instead. You change what you want and how you see things, so let your partner change too, or else you are holding them back, which leads to relationship issues.

Be aware of how your partner has been behaving. Look for the signs that something may be going wrong. Your partner won't always tell you when they are worried that something in your relationship or in their personal life is wrong. While it is best to communicate with each other, there are always times when your partner isn't going to talk to you, and you aren't going to talk to them in the way that either of you want. Thus, you should learn the signs of your relationship issues and problems with your partner. Maybe they get extra moody about buying certain luxuries when they're struggling at work. Maybe they become angry when they're having issues with their parents. Whatever their response may be, you can use those responses to determine how to establish a better future with your partner. The more you pick up on the signs, the more you can facilitate better communication.

If your partner seems unhappy, don't wait for them to come to you. You can initiate hard conversations with your partner when you sense there are issues. There's no reason to wait for when your partner finally has the motivation to speak, which may never happen. Sometimes, it takes the burden off one person when the other broaches a topic first. It makes them think, "Oh, my partner wants to have this conversation, so I don't have to bring it up myself, and I can safely say what I need to say." Bad feelings don't do any good when they linger, so take bad feelings you sense, and call them out. Show your partner that you are willing to listen and be there for them, no matter what they are facing. The measure of a good partner is your desire to bring happiness to your significant other while bringing happiness to yourself.

Plan for your future together. Making plans is one of the best ways to be forward-thinking about your future with your partner. Don't be afraid of dreaming about a life with your partner because you're afraid that your relationship might end. Good relationships allow those imaginings of a future together to thrive, and they build those dreams up. When you can dream with your partner, you are telling your subconscious mind that you want to spend a long time with the person you are with; accordingly, your subconscious mind will work on your behalf to make those dreams come true. You'll still have to put in a conscious effort, but your mindset will be wired to reach your goals. If you don't have future ambitions, you become fixated on things you cannot control about the future rather than the dreams that are in your power. Stop fixating on the unknowns and embrace everything that you can create with your mental energy.

Be flexible in your relationship. Plans take you a long way, but you cannot make a plan and expect no variation as you go. Sometimes, you'll have to take detours, and other times, you'll choose to take the scenic route, but in all cases, you'll need to be flexible. There's no reason to go about life with rigidity. When you are rigid, it's normal to be anxious because rigidity closes your mind off to ideas that will help you thrive. When you aren't flexible, you limit yourself and your relationship, which can feel incredibly stifling when you're trying to make your relationship work. Both you and your partner need to be open to the future and what that future can look like. There are some things you cannot imagine now that will be major parts of your future if you let them be, so don't limit yourself based on what you think you'll be like ten years from now.

Talk about your insecurities before they grow. If you're upfront about your insecurities, they can never destroy your relationship. Don't try to run away from your insecurities because you think they make you look pathetic or needy. Those are not words that accurately relate to insecurity. Insecurity is normal, and to one extent or another, everyone faces insecurity in their life, so having them isn't something you should be ashamed of. Your partner also has insecurities, and you wouldn't want to make them feel bad about theirs, so they will likely not make you feel bad about yours, and if they do, you have serious issues in your relationship to work through if you ever want to make it last! When you open about your insecurities, they become less powerful, so stay open about what makes you insecure and ensure that your partner stays open about their insecurities as well.

There will always be times when it's hard to communicate properly with your partner. You'll scratch your head as you try to figure out what they are thinking and wonder if there's something floating between you that needs to be addressed. The key to a good relationship is staying engaged with the other person. Don't fall into a comfortable silence. You cannot be communicative without communicating, so, duh, you need to maintain forms of communication, which don't have to be oral. As long as you are honest with one another and check-in with each other, you shouldn't have much to worry about.

Complete Projects Together

Find common interests with your partner. When you work on projects together, you invest combined resources to complete a finished project that belongs to both of you. Projects are an investment in a relationship because they give you something to share. They set aside your differences, and they allow you to bond over a common interest. Additionally, they are reminders of why you need to keep fighting for your relationship. They show you that there is something worth fighting for and that no matter how different you are, there are things that you have in common with your partner. Additionally, projects give you time to talk as you put your bodies to use for something more significant than yourselves.

Try home improvement projects together. If you own a home or have an apartment that you can do little projects in, doing home improvement projects as a team can be a great idea. When you do this, you're both having a say in what your home looks like, and you are both putting physical and mental labor into the process. You are investing in your relationship, and when you invest in something, you are less likely to back out because of fear. You don't have to be crafty to do minor home improvement projects. Even just rearranging a room can transform your space and make you both feel more at home. When you work on your home together, you can combine your lives and include elements that you both love, which is so much better than one person making the majority of decorating decisions.

Get active with your partner. Incorporating more physical activity with your partner is another way to bond. You don't have to do anything as intense as going to the gym with your partner or going for a run, but little active acts such as going for a walk or a hike can help you connect with your significant others in new ways. When you participate in these activities, you detach from all your other commitments, and you take time to be present in the moment. This presence is inevitably felt by your partner, who will feel good when they have your attention. As you engage in walking, or whatever else you choose to do, you can talk and take time away from your busy lives. Health projects are just as valid as any other ones.

Plan a big project that will take years to complete. When you choose a project that will take a while to complete, you are saying, "I believe in us, and I want to put that time in. I believe we're going to make it, so I'm not afraid of what will happen if we don't." You're showing that you have faith in your relationship, enough faith to dedicate your future to actions you'll be doing with your partner. Taking out a loan for a house and renovating it is a serious commitment for a couple to make, but it validates the relationship and can add a sense of security for partners. Big projects allow you to halve the amount of effort you must put into your huge dreams, which is a blessing you can only get when you put your heart into your relationship.

Use your strengths to benefit one another. Everyone has unique abilities that can be beneficial during a huge project that requires extensive effort. You each have different abilities that make you fit for completing various tasks. Adding your skills together makes your flaws less profound, and it allows you to get more accomplished in the same amount of time. Don't try to handle a project all by yourself when you know that you could benefit from your partner's skills. Use that moment as a chance to become closer together and to continue building the relationship you have already established and fought for.

When you complete projects with your partner, you commit to a life together. You show your partner that you want to put time into them and with them, and you show yourself that you're not going to run away from your relationship. You're going to commit to the future you want, and you're going to hope that everything turns out for the best. You can't know what will happen in the future, so the best you can do is have faith that whatever happens will be something amazing.

Visible Actions of Love Matter

You have to show your partner that you love them, and this idea may seem basic, but many partners lose track of visible actions of love as their relationship progresses. They start to think, "They know that I love them," but they may not know if you do not show them. Saying "I love you" is good, but you also have to show your affection or your partner will start to sense mixed signals. For some people, this kind of affection is hard to show, and it makes them feel so vulnerable and afraid, but it important for the health of you and your partner to incorporate these acts more often. When you add them to your love life, your partner feels more secure, which reduces anxiety.

Physical affection often makes your partner feel more loved. Acts such as kissing, hugging, and cuddling can make your partner feel cared for. If you don't do these acts or stop doing them, your partner may get the sense that you are withdrawing emotionally from the relationship, and they may start to think that you do not care for them in the way they care for you. Physical touch is not for everyone, and some couples do not like it much. Still, it is an essential facet of relationships for many people, so ensuring that you meet your partner's physical connection needs is vital. Everyone likes different forms of physical touch, so respond to what your partner likes, and avoid what makes them uncomfortable, and they should do the same for you.

Sexual intimacy is something that society doesn't always address, but for some people, it is highly important. While some couples may have no or little interest in sex, sexual intimacy is a great way for two people to become closer and give them comfort and love. Your sexuality is an important part of you, and you cannot avoid that side of yourself altogether. You need to engage in consensual acts with your partner, of course, but you shouldn't feel the need to hide your sexual side or be ashamed of it. Sex can help people feel closer to one another, and when a couple who loves to have sex together doesn't do it as much, they can start to feel a disconnect that leaves people feeling insecure. Thus, you have to take a look at your sex life and decide what will give you inner peace and relationship security.

Do little things like giving them flowers, which serve as reminders of your love. Little acts keep your love life flourishing because they serve as daily reminders that your relationship is strong and can survive whatever life throws at you. You should show your love daily. Anything like leaving notes or clearing the snow from their care can communicate love. Thus, going just a little out of your way for your partner can make a significant impact on your relationship. Don't be afraid to be affectionate around your partner and to show how much you love them.

Express Your Feelings

You can't just share your feelings once and be done with sharing them because feelings aren't static. They come and go, and they adapt to your circumstances. Feelings are something that you're going to have to keep up with for the rest of your life. Many times, you won't know what to do with them. You'll feel a bubble of something in the pit of your stomach, and it will be hard to know what to make of it. You'll wonder if the feelings you have will ever go away because it's confusing to have them there all the time. Feelings are here to stay, and if you make the best of them, they are a good thing. They allow you to connect with the world and feel joy. If you're open about them and embrace them, they will do more good than harm.

Find a friend who can help you think through your feelings. Sometimes, you need to discuss your feelings with someone who isn't your partner. While you want to be open with your partner, you often need to process what you are feeling first before you can try explaining it to your partner. A friend is a great source for when you're worried about how your partner may react to your feelings or when you want an outside view to help guide you and give you clarity. Find a friend you can trust to be fair and understand with your feelings without casting too many judgments. You probably have a friend who is a born listener. They are a great choice.

Use an activity to express your feelings. Often, it helps people to get active and use their bodies to show how they are feeling. There are so many outlets you can use to express your feeling. Dancing to a song that makes you emotional is one choice, or you write a creative story. Doing art is another good option. Whatever helps you release your emotions will do. You don't have to be "good" at whatever you choose to do. If you think you suck at art, but it feels good, do it! Don't limit yourself based on your talent level. Art is found in so many ways, and there's a way to express yourself that is all yours and can't be ruined by what critics would say.

Don't be passive-aggressive. When you're passive-aggressive, you're avoiding your feelings by trying to redirect them. You're acting like you're fine, when really you're feeling the opposite. Leaving little sticky notes for your partner while acting unbothered by whatever it is they did that irritated you is no way to express feelings. Passive aggression keeps the aggression bottled up inside you. It can have temporary results, but it will not make you feel better in the long term because it does not solve anything. Passive aggression takes your anger, it traps it within you, which is toxic to your emotional health.

Show your feelings in your actions and your words. You need to be consistent with what you say and what you do. When you say, "I am fine," but you look upset, your partner will not know how you are really feeling. This concept has the same downsides of passive aggression, and it can turn into passive-aggressive behaviors. Your actions and your words will always have some disconnect because you cannot be fully self-aware, and you won't always know how you are feeling, but when you are honest with yourself, you can give more consistent signals to your partner, which will make life easier for both of you.

Stop being afraid of your feelings. Feelings are scary, but they can only harm you when you give them the power to hurt you. Empower yourself to live with your feelings rather than trying to numb yourself. When you numb yourself, you lose your connection to your personality, and you become a hollow version of yourself, which is no way to be if you want your partner to feel secure (or yourself). Whether they are bad or good, allow yourself to feel what you are feeling because you cannot control your feelings, but you feed energies into them and give them chances to change for the better.

Your feelings are going to stay long after you have fixed your relationship anxiety, and if you don't continue to be honest about them, you'll find yourself back where you started. You don't want to have wasted all the time you put in fighting your anxiety. Once you have gotten through the worst of your anxiety, you'll want to continue on the positive path you're on, so be true with your feelings, and even when you feel calm, stay in touch with them because if you don't, anxiety will come back stronger than ever.

Compliment Your Partner

Your partner needs to know that you believe in them, and if they think that you doubt certain parts of them or don't like the way they are, they might start to feel insecure. People need affirmation from time to time. They need to be validated, and this need for validation isn't a weakness. It's merely part of being alive and trying to get a sense of the world. When you ignore your partner's achievements or when you feel proud of them, you're missing out on opportunities to make them feel good and appreciated, which leads to trouble down the line. Don't just applaud them for big things like a promotion at work. Show them that you are complimentary of even little things like a good meal.

Try to find something nice to say about your partner each day. When you learn to appreciate your partner each day, you show your love. Appreciating what a person can do and the personal decision they make is better than just appreciating how they look or other things they cannot control. For example, don't say, "You look hot today," which might be taken well by your partner but has no real reflection on their skills. Saying something like, "The way you put together your outfit is nice, and it shows your personality well," goes beyond just physicality and compliments your partner's expressive skills. Compliments don't have to be generic. Find unique ways to show your appreciation. Make an offhanded comment about how you wish you could do something as well as you can. You can compliment someone daily without it becoming cheesy or trite. The more you show your appreciation, the less awkward it will feel.

Compliment them on more than just what they look like. Your partner is more than their looks. They're not just a handsome or pretty face, and if you only compliment what they look like, you're missing out on so much, and you may be putting too much emphasis on looks. With too much emphasis on looks, your partner may feel pressure to go to an extreme to look the way you want, and they can hurt themselves in the process. One man, Kye started weight lifting for hours a day because he thought his girlfriend, Jilly, wanted him to be more buff. He became so obsessed with gaining muscle that he lost track of his relationship. Jilly didn't want a super buff boyfriend more than a present boyfriend!

When you feel the need to be critical, try being complimentary instead. If you want to make a comment about how your partner is deficient, try to think of something positive instead, and if you must give constructive criticism, sandwich that criticism between things that you think they did well. Complimenting someone isn't flattery, and it shouldn't be disingenuine. Rather, it is a more positive way of looking at situations. Being overly critical is always bad for a relationship because it makes the other person fell lie they can never please you, but when you add a health mix of compliments, the relationship feels more balanced.

Be genuine with your compliments. Don't say anything for the mere sake of saying it because doing so makes your compliments feel fake, which makes your partner feel like you're just pitying them. When you honestly compliment your partner, they feel loved, and you reassure their insecurities.

Love in New Ways

Find new ways to express your love as you continue to fight your relationship anxiety because you cannot always express your love in the same ways. The old ways of loving have failed you. They have made you more anxious, and they almost prevented you from entering the future with your partner. You need to find new ways to engage and communicate with your partner. It's fun to be in a partnership because a partnership is a constant opportunity for exploration and development. Each day is a new chance to do better and love in new ways. Don't think of loving in new ways as something scary, but look it as an adventure that will make you fall even more in love.

Love the little things of being in a partnership because those are things that bring you inner peace. It's the little things like waking up on a sunny morning to the sun shining on your partner's sleeping face, or smelling the breakfast your partner is making wafting into your bedroom that make you feel like you're still in love. It is the goodnight kisses and the watching movies on a Saturday afternoon that feel so good but are often parts of your life that you take advantage of. Love is so much so in the little things, and it is the joy you find in the ordinary. It is seeing a flawed person and thinking that they are exactly what you need. Your love is dynamic and vibrant, so start looking at it that way because love is the best feeling you'll ever have.

Know that while grand gestures are nice, your partner will enjoy having a smooth, day to day relationship over those grand gestures. It's better to take the trash out once in a while than to buy your partner an expensive gift that they'll forget about when the trash is full and their responsibility for the hundredth time in a row. You don't have to spend any money to show your love. While little gifts can have sentimental value, you can also love by your actions. Take that garbage out or clean the bathroom. Make dinner one night not because it is your turn but because you what to give your partner a break.

Challenge the norms of your relationship—the expectations of who should do what shouldn't be forced. If circumstances change, make changes in how your household is run. Julie and Brian struggled to adapt to how they dealt with household duties after Brian was let go from his job. Brian was at home more, but Julie was still doing all the old household duties that she had before, and she was feeling exhausted, so because of their new circumstances, Brian took it upon himself to learn to cook for his wife and three children. He began to clean more and took care of more of the household duties while looking for his job. Jule and Brian are a great example of how you have to adapt to how your love life functions as life throws obstacles at you. What was normal once upon a time doesn't have to be normal anymore.

The plan doesn't always bring you happiness. What you planned for your future won't always be what you want for your future, so you should be view your plans as a guideline not as a prophecy of what needs to happen. You can change your mind, and your partner can change their mind. Be open to new opportunities, and when you see a chance, you should take it. By taking opportunities, your love life may change, and you'll have to shift how you love your partner, but you can love your partner just as profoundly, even if circumstances require you to show your love in new ways.

Love isn't easy, and it doesn't happen how you expect, but that's part of the fun.

When you find new ways to love your partner, you add excitement and hope to your relationship, so your relationship can be resilient and calm even in hard times. Learn to love in new ways so your partnership can thrive into the uncertain future.

CHAPTER 11

Resolve your Differences

This book has been full of advice, teaching you how to be more communicative and kind to your partner to resolve your relationship anxiety. It can be overwhelming with all that information, but here are a few final tips that can bring all the advice together and give you some of the key takeaways of this book. If you hold onto nothing else, hold onto these final pieces of advice that can be beneficial in any relationship.

Be Supportive and More Forgiving

Showing support and forgiveness can be hard when you have grievances against your partner. You'll want to withhold both those things when you're upset with your partner. Under such circumstances, you feel a hot pit of raging feelings in your stomach, and you aren't sure what to do about them, so you turn them onto your relationship. You may be so angry that you are tempted to turn against your partner and hold them responsible for all the bad feelings that you have and everything that goes wrong with your life. Partners can too quickly become scapegoat, and when you scapegoat them, you jeopardize your relationship with your partner, and you send them the message that they can do nothing right. Sometimes, your partner will wrong you, but you cannot hold their mistakes against them forever if you want to move forward. Holding onto all those bad feelings fuels your anxiety, and the more they amplify in your head, the harder it becomes to think clearly. You have to learn them to support your partner even when it is hard and forgive the wrongs they do against you.

You would want forgiveness, so give it to your partner. If you want your partner to be merciful to you, you have to be merciful to them. It can be hard to suck up your pride and extend that forgiveness to someone who has hurt you, but if they haven't hurt you enough that you want the relationship to end, they haven't hurt you enough for you to hold a grudge either. Forgiveness isn't just about giving something to your partner. It is about giving a chance to yourself as well because when you offer forgiveness, you open yourself up to being hurt rather than putting an iron wall around yourself that keeps all emotions out of your life.

You would also want support, so when something means a lot to your partner, you need to support them in their endeavors. Support doesn't mean begrudgingly letting them go on a fun outing with friends you don't like much. You cannot begrudge them and still support them because support requires you to be gracious and glad that your partner is doing actions that make them happy. If you give your approval and then hold a grudge, you are being passive-aggressive rather than showing support, and as you know, being passive-aggressive is pretty toxic. Support doesn't mean condoning inappropriate behavior, but it does mean encouraging your partner to be happy and healthy. When you support your partner, they are more willing to support you, which creates an equal dynamic.

Don't withhold support or forgiveness because you are jealous. Jealousy never gets a person very far in a relationship, and anxiety is encouraged by such feelings. If you're jealous of the attention your partner is giving to another person or a thing (such as their work), it's not right to avoid those feelings you have. You can't send your partner the message of, "I support you," while really hoping that they fail an endeavor so that their attention comes back to you. That's petty and not the actions of a loving partner who wants to make a relationship work. Be genuine with your support and your forgiveness because if you aren't, there's no point in pretending that you're a caring partner. If your motives for "support" are selfish, that's not true support, and you need to look inward and see if you are giving your partner real support or conditional support based on your insecurities and worries.

Refusing support doesn't make you feel any better. Holding back your support isn't going to make you feel better about yourself. You'll see your partner hurting, and you may get temporary vindication, but your relationship won't be better for it, so you'll never truly feel better. Petty actions are just a bandaid for your problems. They cover them up, but they don't heal them. When you refuse to be supportive, you are fundamentally withdrawing from the relationship before it has even ended. You don't have to support people who don't support you or who hurt you, but in a relationship, you have to support your partner or end the relationship. Otherwise, you are continuing the relationship under false pretenses.

Being bitter only hurts you. It may hurt your partner too, but at the end of the day, your partner is going to get over your bitterness (unless they form their own bitterness), and they'll move on without you. Animosity leaves you alone, and it makes you a shell of your normal self. You don't feel happy when you feel resentful because you cannot see the good in the world. You become a victim who has been hurt rather than an individual who can push through hardships. Don't let yourself drown in your resentment because if you do, you may lose someone important to you. It hurts to be betrayed, but it hurts more to hold onto betrayal.

Forgiveness and support are essential parts of relationships. If you cannot do either of these things, your relationship probably won't improve because withdrawing support and clutching onto resentment create a rift between you and your partner. They make you unable to see the good parts of your significant other, and they create tension that is hard to correct. They fill you with even more anxiety, and they make it nearly impossible to understand your own feelings.

Knowing If Your Relationship is Worth It

You may be wondering, now that you have gone through this book, "Is my relationship worth it?" Some relationships may not seem like they are worth saving. You may be so far into an anxiety hole that even all the methods in this book seem like they cannot help you. It's hard to admit that a relationship may need to end, and naturally, you don't want to give up all the time, energy, and love you put into your relationship, but in some cases, anxiety can't be fixed in a relationship because one or both partners no longer are committed to making the relationship work, or the relationship is too toxic or abusive to fix. Some relationships aren't right, and that okay. I don't want you to fight for something that hurts you, so use the following questions to determine if your relationship is right for you.

Does your relationship bring you internal peace? If your relationship brings you some kind of internal peace. If the good parts make you feel calm and in control, that's a good sign, but be honest with what inner peace means to you. Inner peace is not being filled with relief when you've stopped fighting with your partner for just a little while. If you feel good because you have a reprieve from the chaos, that is not true inner peace. True inner peace is a feeling of overall contentment with your partner despite hardships in your relationship. They still give you comfort even if you're unable to be there for each other as much as you used to.

Is it hard to imagine a happy life without your partner? If you struggle to imagine yourself being happy without your partner, you're either truly in love and committed or you have attachment issues. But beyond attachment issues, I'm talking about the feeling of aching to be with someone rather than needing them. While you know you could stand on your feet without them, you would feel less happy doing so without the other person your life. That feeling is what you want in a relationship. You can be independent while still yearning to have a person forever in your life because of how important they are to you.

Are there more pros than cons? If there are more good parts of your relationship than bad parts, that's a good sign. If you find yourself stacking up a list of cons, you may just be in a mental headspace, but you also may just be unhappy with the relationship beyond just your anxiety. Anxiety can cast a big shadow over a relationship, making it hard to see the good, but if you are conscious in your efforts to be honest about what you don't like and what you like about your relationship, you'll start to uncover how you truly feel. If even with anxiety, your relationship has more pros than cons, it's likely worth fighting for that relationship.

Are you ready to go through some challenging conversations? You'll have lots of hard conversations during the duration of any relationship. If you're ready to dive into some hard to process conversations, then you're in a good mindset to continue your relationship. If you aren't prepared to endure some conversations that make you uncomfortable, your relationship might not be worth it to you. For any relationship to work, you have to be ready to go through struggles with grace and strength. If you're unwilling to do that, you're not going to get anywhere, so you might as well end the relationship before you have any more heartache.

Can you love your partner as they are? If you cannot love your partner as they are right now, then there's no hope that you will ever love them in the way a person deserves to be loved, and that's not fair to either of you. While you can dislike a person's behaviors, you cannot find their core character traits irredeemable and still claim to love and be committed to a continued relationship with them. In a relationship, you have to choose to love someone and keep loving them even though they have flaws that you know you'll never change. People are who they are, and you can't force them to be different no matter how much you work on your relationship.

Do you think your partner can love you as you are? Your partner needs to love you just as you are, just as you need to love them just as you are. You may like to think that you can change yourself to suit what your partner wants, but if you try to change yourself, you will always feel anxiety. You will start to wonder if you can ever be good enough for your partner. You will feel like a fraud because you're trying to be the person you think your partner wants rather than yourself. If your partner will never love you when you are genuinely yourself, they are not a partner who is a good fit for you, and you need to move on for both of your well-beings.

Does your partner treat you with respect? Partnerships are all about respect, and respect can be built, but if your partner does not even try to respect you, then they may not be committed to giving what they need to give into the relationship, and disrespect also can be an indicator that your partner wants to change you and struggles to love you are. You deserve respect and affection, so if your partner repetitively doesn't give you those things, you may want to move on. If your partner respects despite miscommunication and anxiety issues, they may be a keeper!

Do you treat your partner with respect? If your partner causes you to act in toxic ways, it may be time to move on. If you find that your partner brings out the worst in you, and you are not treating your partner with respect, you are the problem in the relationship, and you are not a good fit for the other person. You'll never be in a strong relationship with someone you can't respect. It doesn't matter what you don't respect about them; if you don't respect them, your relationship will be filled with worries and insecurities that you'll never give the attention they need to heal.

Are your partner's goals and yours compatible? While you and your partner may be compatible in every way imaginable, if your wishes for the future aren't compatible, you may not be able to make things work between you. For example, Taylor and Jay were divided over whether they wanted to have kids. Taylor didn't want to be a parent while their partner, Jay, wanted to be a parent more than anything. They couldn't continue their relationship because they had different dreams of what they wanted from their partner. They were sad to end the relationship, but they couldn't meet each other halfway because they wanted opposite things. Sometimes, it's time to end things, even when they make you happy.

Do you and your partner still love each other? If you and your partner still love each other, that's a great sign that you can get through your hardship. Love cannot save a relationship, but it is a fundamental building block for any relationship. Suppose you honestly don't love your partner and don't think that you'll ever love them romantically. In that case, it's not fair to either of you to keep the relationship going without additional transparency and communicating what you want out of the relationship. You shouldn't make your partner think you love them if you don't because it's unfair to mess with people's feelings like that.

Are you holding onto the relationship because it's important to you rather than staying because you are afraid of life outside the relationship? If you're holding onto something that is valuable to you, then yes, it is good to fight for that thing, but if you're only holding on because the world outside your relationship is scary, you need to reevaluate your relationship. When you've been in a relationship for a while, you can be dependent on it, which makes you resistant to leaving that relationship even if it isn't making you happy anymore. Don't hold onto something for mere sentimentality or because you're afraid of being alone. Holding onto a relationship that isn't good for you only makes it harder to start the right relationship.

Are you secure in your role as an individual in your relationship? If you feel lost in the influence of another person, your relationship may be compromised. You need to feel confident in your individuality when you're in a relationship. While feeling lost in your partner's identity doesn't mean you immediately need to bail on your relationship, it does mean that you need to do more self-reflection and learn if you're relying on your relationship for a sense of identity. You need to know who you are without your partner's influence, which may mean that you need to take some time away from the relationship to figure out who you are.

Is your future with the other person a healthy one? If you cannot envision a future in which you are happy and healthy with a person, you may have problems that run much deeper than your anxiety. In such cases, your anxiety may be based on your instincts and red flags that you've found in your relationship. You should never sacrifice your general mental, physical, or spiritual health because of your relationship. You need to be healthy if you don't want anxiety to take over your entire life. Additionally, if you cannot see your partner ever being healthy with you, that's also a red flag that you should consider. Both partners in a relationship need to be healthy in all areas of health, and if the relationship somehow prohibits that, relationship anxiety will always persist. In such cases, you can either address why you or your partner can't be healthy as things are, or you can choose to end the relationship because you don't think you or your partner could ever make the changes you need to make.

Are you ready to fight for your relationship? If you're ready to fight for your relationship, that is the best sign that your relationship is a good fit. When you're willing to put the work into your relationship, you are more likely to get what you want out of it, and you are more likely to put anxiety in its place for good. If you've got a fighting spirit, your relationship can survive as long as it is healthy for both you and your partner. Most obstacles you can get over with a little patience and a good deal of time.

If you answer yes to these questions, your relationship could have what it needs to recover from the cracks that anxiety has put in it. Relationships are more resilient than they are fragile. They often seem delicate, but that is because people often tiptoe around them rather than confronting the issues they have. They try to avoid conflict when conflict and asking yourself hard questions is often required for good relationships to develop into great ones. Be honest with yourself about your answers to these questions and the nature of your relationship. The more open you are about your experiences now, the less pain you'll have in the future.

Consult with a Professional

When you have extreme problems, you may need to seek professional help. Some issues are too complex to handle alone, and if you and your partner struggle to get on the same page, a mental health professional or a relationship expert can give you the guidance and nudges you need to take care of your issues. Lots of couples seek professional help, and for many, it is beneficial. Not everyone has the resources to seek help, but if you have them and cannot seem to take the steps in this book alone, an expert might be the very person to save your relationship. A professional can serve as an intermediary who can help you and your partner see eye to eye.

Talking to a professional shouldn't make you feel ashamed. There's nothing wrong with needing outside help. Most people could benefit from it every so often. One couple, Brad and Ella, moved to a new state and they didn't have a big support system in their new state, so they both benefitted from having a counselor, who served as a third-party for them and helped the couple start having more civil conversations and reigniting their passion for each other. Even if you haven't moved across the country, you may benefit from having someone outside your normal life who can help you and your partner.

If you or your partner has mental health issues, a professional intermediary can be helpful and teach you to work on your joint and individual issues. Experts can give you specialized exercise for the main issues in your relationship, and they show you how to build coping skills to resist your anxiety. These skills can be useful beyond just your immediate relationship. They can help you better your overall mental health, which is also good for your relationship as a whole.

Choose a professional who specializes in relationship counseling or any specific needs you have. Don't just go to the first person you see on the list of mental health experts. Choose someone who specializes in whatever it is you need. If you're looking for someone who deals with a disorder such as borderline personality disorder and relationships, for example, see if any available clinicians know both areas. Doing your research can maximize your therapeutic experience, and finding the right person for your issues can be the difference between success and failure.

It can take time to find a professional who works for your needs. Take your time when deciding who you want to turn to. Some professionals won't vibe well with you, but don't get discouraged; there's probably someone out there who is more fit for your needs. You need to find a professional who you feel comfortable talking to, and your partner feels comfortable talking to as well. Once you find someone you like, dedicate yourself to their care and listen to what they tell you because they likely know better than you.

Fight for Your Relationship

If you want to make your relationship work, you need to fight for your relationship because hoping for change is not enough. Fighting for your relationship will require some physical energy, but it will mostly require emotional energy. Right now, you'll feel like you're a ball trying to roll up a hill. It will feel like it requires so much just to face the anxiety, but soon, you will realize that you can stand up on your feet and walk up that hill, even if it feels like torture to do so at times. The destination will be well worth the struggle because you will save your relationship from the anxiety that fragments it. If you and your partner work together, you'll make progress in no time.

You need to understand what causes anxiety in your relationship. Learn the causes of anxiety in your relationship and challenge them. Communicate those worries and realize that they might not have a rational place in your life. Accept the feelings of anxiety that you have, but do not give into them. When you know your anxiety's roots, it's hard to take anxiety seriously because you logically know what that anxiety is a product. Some anxiety is deeply buried over layers of lies you've told yourself and others. You've avoided the truth for long enough. It's time to embrace it, no matter what it is, and urge your partner to embrace their truth too.

You must identify the obstacles that make it hard to overcome your anxiety. Know why you're having such a hard time dealing with your anxiety, and all the things that worsen your anxiety. Discuss these obstacles with your partner. Once you know your problems, you can begin to address them through working on yourself and your relationship. Take your issues one at a time, and learn to overcome them gradually. You'll get overwhelmed if you try to handle everything at once, so take it as slowly as you need to. Healing your relationship isn't a race, so you have all the time you need to do it if you're willing to commit the time.

As you work through your relationship issues, you should create a sense of security in your relationship. Ensure that you create an emotional and physical environment that feels safe for both you and your partner. If something makes your partner uncomfortable but helps make you feel secure, try to find a compromise that can serve you both. For example, Jeff liked to keep a gun in the bedroom, and his wife, Kelsi wanted the weapon out of the house altogether. They finally agreed that Jeff could keep a small gun safe in the gun, but it was not appropriate for their bedroom. While they still don't see eye to eye on guns, they found a way to both feel secure in their house and to make peace with one another as well.

Become self-aware, and learn to deal with your feelings, and give them the due that they deserve. Start to realize your part in the relationship anxiety that plagues your relationship. Be honest with yourself, and know how you contribute to some of your relationship issues. When you understand how you influence your anxiety or your partner's you can address it more pragmatic away without shutting down emotionally. You will always be anxious if you don't get self-aware. Self-awareness can require realizing some hard truths and addressing parts of yourself that you don't particularly like. Still, it is an essential part of the process of getting rid of your relationship anxiety.

Reconnect with your partner and your relationship. Take the time to bridge your gaps whenever you start to feel that you are growing distant. You should never feel like you don't know your partner. Romantic relationships are some of the closest relationships that you have, and they often lead to people spending most of their lives together, and that means that you need to know your partner and continue to get to know them. Don't assume that you know how they are feeling or what they want just because you know more about them than anyone. When you listen to your partner, how they feel, and what they want may surprise you.

Learn to communicate better and be vulnerable. Communication is a vital part of any relationship. If you do not have communication skills, you have no hope of rising above you or your partner's anxiety. Allow yourself to have open communication and reassure your partner that it is safe for them to communicate openly with you. The more you practice healthy communication, the easier it becomes to be vulnerable, and the better you'll feel. Anxiety cannot live while you communicate your needs and your concerns. Put anxiety on blast by being as honest and open as you can with your partner. It is scary to communicate, but it's not as hard as you probably fear when you do it.

Be more compassionate for yourself and your partner. Compassion is one of the most important lessons you can learn to improve your relationship. When you have understanding, you act with empathy and kindness. You see beyond your selfish needs, and you learn to respect you and your partner. If you don't respect yourself or your partner, you are never going to have an anxiety-free relationship because disrespect towards one part of a relationship is disrespectful to the entire thing. You need to let your heart dive into your relationship, and allow it to be a deeper part of everything you do in that relationship. Logic can be great, but it is not everything, and sometimes, you have to feel what your heart is saying above all else, which is the best way to be more compassionate.

Maintain the lessons you have learned for the rest of your life because they will guide you, and they will help you fight to the end for the relationship you crave. Even if your relationship ends, these lessons can help you in any relationship you have. They show you how to fight for your future and hold onto a vital relationship that makes you feel alive. Relationships are never easy, and they can leave you heartbroken, but they are well worth the risk, and without love, you feel hollow. You lose one of the most vital parts of human life. Let yourself fall in love, and teach yourself how to stay in love. Love is the most rewarding part of human life, so fight for that love, and let it fill you with new feelings, even when your love has grown old.

www.ingramcontent.com/pod-product-compliance
Lightning Source LLC
Chambersburg PA
CBHW071825080526
44589CB00012B/922